Dún Aonghasa

· · · · · · · · · · · · · · · · · · · ·

THE GUIDEBOOK

THE DISCOVERY PROGRAMME LTD.,
63 Merrion Square, Dublin 2, Ireland.
www.discoveryprogramme.ie

ISBN 978-0-9536973-1-1

Text: Claire Cotter
Layout: Ian McCarthy
Design: Claire Cotter & Ian McCarthy

The Discovery Programme would like to acknowledge
the financial assistance received from the
Department of Arts, Heritage and the Gaeltacht towards
the writing of this guidebook.

Printed in Northern Ireland
by GPS Colour Graphics Ltd.,
Alexander Road, Belfast BT69HP, Northern Ireland.

Contents

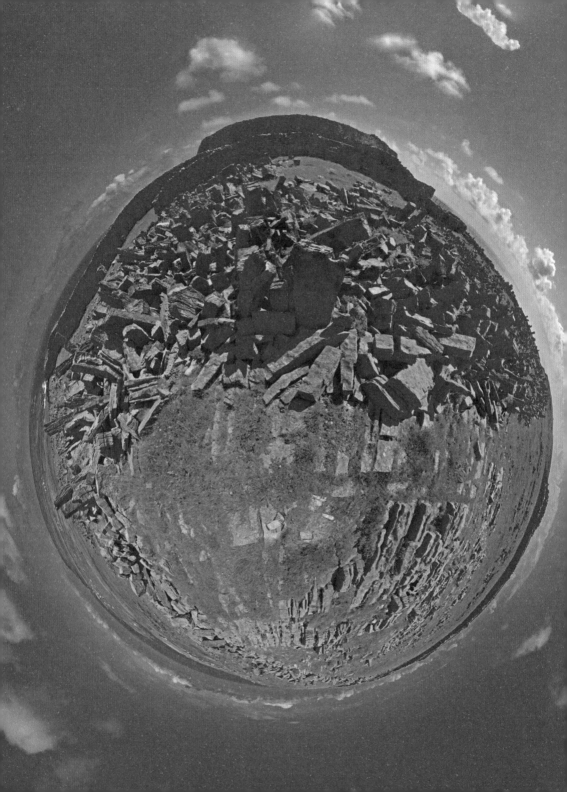

Preface

Dún Aonghasa, Aran Islands, Co. Galway is one of the most spectacularly sited Irish National Monuments. You may be reading this guidebook because you are planning a visit to the fort. Perhaps you are already there. Wherever you are, we hope you enjoy reading it.

The book provides lots of information on the life and times of the people who built the first fort on the hilltop around 1000 BC and those who rebuilt it on an even more impressive scale over 1500 years later. The nineteenth century antiquarians who agitated - successfully - for the conservation of the fort also deserve a mention.

The information is based on archaeological excavations, directed by the author, that took place in the fort between 1992 and 1995. The results of those investigations were published in two volumes in 2013 (see 'Further Reading' at the end of the guidebook). Here the main findings are presented in a more accessible form.

Dún Aonghasa is a National Monument that has been in state care since the late nineteenth century. It is one of seven large stone forts on the Aran Islands cared for by a partnership of the National Monument Services of the Department of Arts, Heritage and the Gaeltacht and the Office of Public Works. You can help to preserve these monuments and their landscapes for future generations by not walking on the fragile drystone walls, removing or throwing down stones, or building little stone 'pyramids' on the landscape.

The Discovery Programme
Centre for Irish
Archaeological Research

The excavations at Dún Aonghasa and Dún Eoghanachta (a second smaller fort lying 2km to the west) were carried out by The Discovery Programme, Centre for Irish Archaeological Research funded by the Government of Ireland through The Heritage Council of Ireland.

Timeline

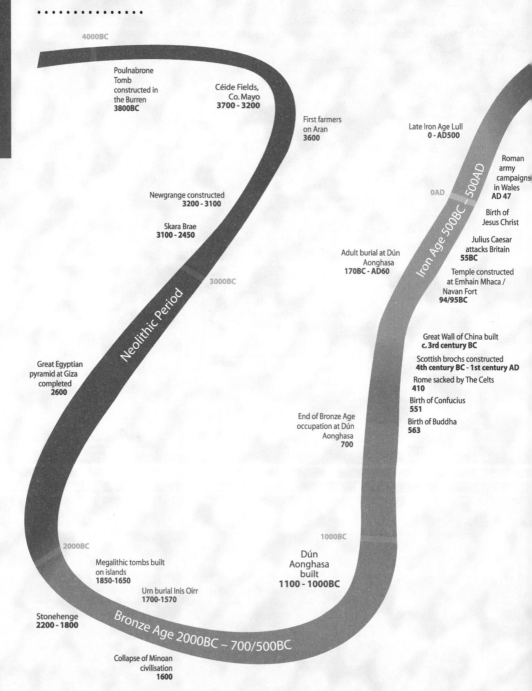

4000BC

Poulnabrone
Tomb
constructed in
the Burren
3800BC

Céide Fields,
Co. Mayo
3700 - 3200

First farmers
on Aran
3600

Late Iron Age Lull
0 - AD500

0AD

Roman
army
campaigns
in Wales
AD 47

Birth of
Jesus Christ

Julius Caesar
attacks Britain
55BC

Temple constructed
at Emhain Mhaca /
Navan Fort
94/95BC

Newgrange constructed
3200 - 3100

Skara Brae
3100 - 2450

Adult burial at Dún
Aonghasa
170BC - AD60

Iron Age 500BC – 500AD

3000BC

Neolithic Period

Great Wall of China built
c. 3rd century BC

Scottish brochs constructed
4th century BC - 1st century AD

Rome sacked by The Celts
410

Birth of Confucius
551

Birth of Buddha
563

Great Egyptian
pyramid at Giza
completed
2600

End of Bronze Age
occupation at Dún
Aonghasa
700

1000BC

2000BC

Megalithic tombs built
on islands
1850-1650

Dún
Aonghasa
built
1100 - 1000BC

Urn burial Inis Oírr
1700-1570

Stonehenge
2200 - 1800

Bronze Age 2000BC – 700/500BC

Collapse of Minoan
civilisation
1600

Éanna founds a
monastery at Cill
Éinne (Killeaney)
600

Colmán Mac Commáin, Bishop of
Munster, dies on Aran
751

Early Medieval Period 500AD – 1000AD

Birth of Mohammed
570

east of
ara last
eld
60

Book of Kells written
800

Dún Aonghasa rebuilt,
Dún Eoghanachta built
c. 800

t. Patrick
rrives in
eland
D 432

Vikings attack the monastery of
Roscam in Galway Bay
807

1000AD

Clare king killed in battle with Connemara
men at Port Chiaráin, Inis Mór
1016

Éanna's monastery is burnt
1020

Battle of Clontarf
1014

Medieval Period 1000 – 1600

The seat of the Munster kings, the
Rock of Cashel, given to the church
1101

Donnchadh O'Brien 'of Aran', the first O'Brien to
bear this title, dies
1120

Connachta erect a fortification, Dún
Gaillimh in Galway
1124

Diarmuid O'Brien rewarded for keeping Galway Bay
free of pirates
1277

Anglo-Norman invasion of Ireland
1169

The Aran Islands described as full of galleys
to plunder English ships
1400

The town of Galway is walled
1250 -70

Mahon O'Brien is killed by his kinsmen at his
castle in Cill Éinne
c.1585

Dissolution of the monasteries
1540s

The O'Flahertys of Connemara take control of
the islands
c.1600

Spanish Armada ships wrecked off the
west coast of Ireland
1588

Áircín fort garrisoned by Cromwellian soldiers
1652-1664

Post-Medieval Period 1600 – 1800

Roderic O'Flaherty publishes an account
of the islands
1684

Clergy of Galway expelled under the Penal Laws
1698

French Revolution
1789

Irish rebellion
1798

Ordnance Survey map the islands
1837

Antiquarian banquet at Dún Aonghasa
1857

The Great Famine
1845-7

Board of Works restore Aran forts
1884-5

J. M. Synge, playwright, spends time
on the Aran Islands
1898-1902

Irish Celtic Revival

Dún Aonghasa excavations and
opening of Visitor Centre

2000AD

The Aran Islands

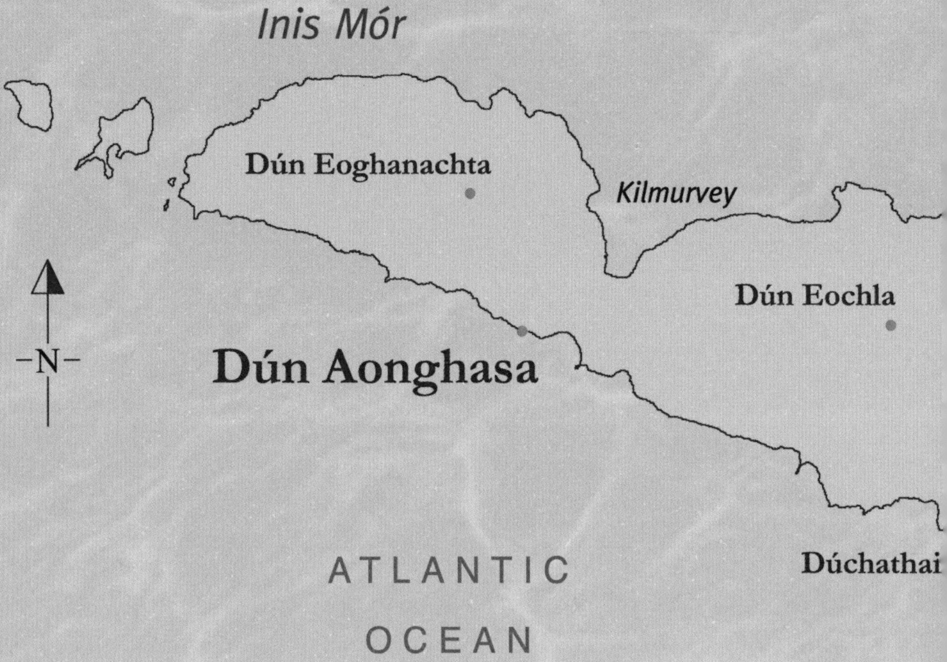

Inis Mór

Dún Eoghanachta

Kilmurvey

Dún Eochla

Dún Aonghasa

Dúchathai

ATLANTIC

OCEAN

-N-

The Aran Islands are Ireland's largest archipelago of inhabited islands and run like a long exclamation mark across the mouth of Galway Bay. They are home to around fourteen hundred people; more than half live on the largest island, Inis Mór. Seven impressively large stone forts are scattered across the islands. The largest, Dún Aonghasa, stands on the cliffs on the southern coast of Inis Mór.

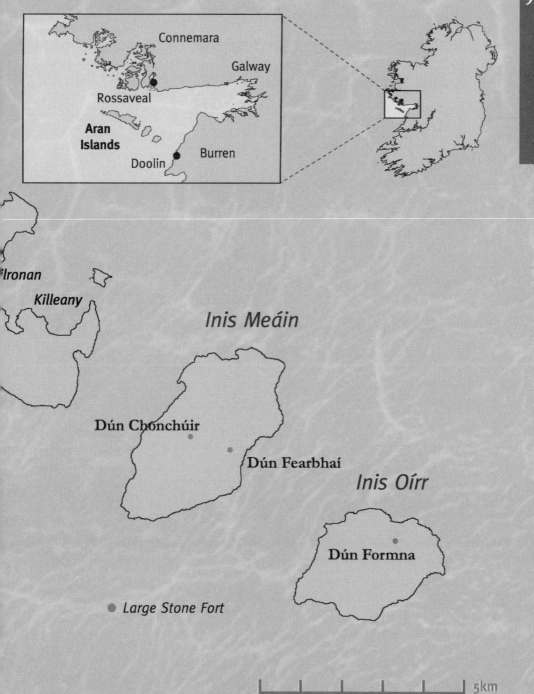

Connemara

Galway

Rossaveal

Aran Islands

Doolin

Burren

Ironan

Killeany

Inis Meáin

Dún Chonchúir

Dún Fearbhaí

Inis Oírr

Dún Formna

Large Stone Fort

5km

Dún Aonghasa

The guidebook takes you on a tour of the fort beginning just outside the 'Modern Entrance'.

Here are a few suggested stops along the way...

1 A good place to view the outer wall stretching away to the cliffs.

2 From here you might just make out the original entrance to the fort on the far right.

3 A good spot to take an initial look at the *chevaux de frise*.

4 The majesty of the looming inner enclosure plus a great view.

5 High terraced walls, enigmatic platform and wall chamber and a cliff-edge location - this is the heart of the fort. People lived here 3000 years ago.

6 The best place to view the *chevaux de frise*.

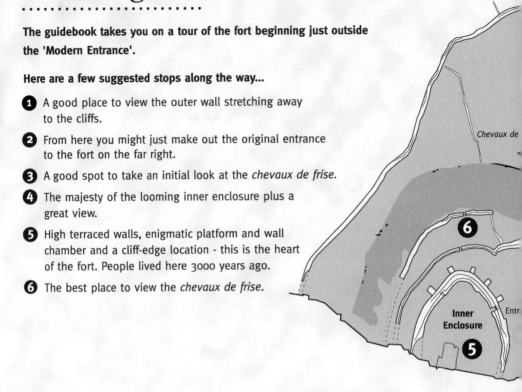

Dún Aonghasa has an area of almost 6 hectares (14 acres). Three curvilinear walls divide the interior into an outer, middle and inner enclosure; all the enclosing walls terminate at the cliff edge. An additional stretch of wall on the western side appears now to be 'hanging in space' but it must have been an integral part of the defences at one time.

Outside the middle enclosure is a cordon of close-set stone pillars (known as a *chevaux de frise*). Even today it is very difficult to pass through this barrier.

The original approach to the fort was from the north, parallel to the limestone terraces, and the earliest entrances in the outer and middle walls face in this direction. The modern route (from the north-east) may date back to the Early Medieval period when there was a monastery at the bottom of the hill where the Visitor Centre now stands.

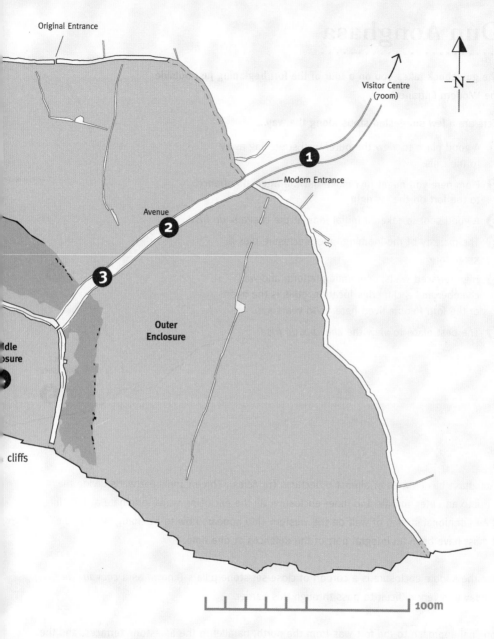

Original Entrance

Visitor Centre
(700m)

-N-

① Modern Entrance

Avenue ②

③

Outer
Enclosure

ddle
osure

cliffs

100m

For a tour based on a 3D survey of the fort scan this QR code
or go to *www.dunaonghasatheguidebook.ie*.

You can use the link to order copies of the guidebook and keep up
to date with ongoing research on stone forts.

The Natural Landscape

Geologically, the Aran Islands are an extension of the limestone region of the Burren, Co. Clare. Terraced slopes, bare rock pavement, thin soil cover and little or no permanent surface water characterise this karst landscape, but there are also many pockets of fertile ground full of sweet grass, herbs and a distinct and diverse flora.

NNE

Inis Mór

SSW

Dún Aonghasa

Dún Aonghasa

Stepped terraces

On the islands, limestone terraces rise from low lying ground at the north shore and end at vertical cliffs facing onto the Atlantic. Dún Aonghasa was built at the highest point of the cliffs.

The Earliest Settlers

The journey from Doolin, in the Burren, to Inis Oírr, is the shortest crossing to the islands and it may well have been this route that brought the first permanent settlers to the islands during the Neolithic (New Stone) age around 5,500 years ago.

Conditions on the islands had certain advantages for early farmers - tree cover was not as dense as in many parts of the mainland. It is doubtful if dangerous wild animals posed a problem.

There were disadvantages too. The islands are a fragile environment, very exposed to Atlantic weather systems and very vulnerable to drought.

Wedge tomb built by early farmers. Dún Aonghasa is just visible in the distance.

Rainwater tanks introduced in the mid-twentieth century make it much easier to water livestock.

Rain is the only source of water and in times of low rainfall, or harsh drying winds, lack of water can be a serious problem.

Writing about the islands in 1684, Roderic O'Flaherty noted that in *'extraordinary dry weather people must turn their cattle out of the islands and the corn fails'.*

What were the islands like when Dún Aonghasa was built?

Sea-levels were lower in the Bronze Age although by how much is debatable - a figure of 6m has been suggested for the southwest of the country. For the islanders, lower sea level meant that there was more land exposed, particularly along the north coast where the waters are relatively shallow.

3D model of Galway Bay

The image is based on recent mapping of the sea-bed. In the bright green areas, water depth is 30m or less. The deep sounds between the islands and the Connemara and Clare coasts rule out the possibility of a land bridge existing in late prehistory, but a journey to the mainland may have involved crossing a number of channels rather than heading into open sea.

The Shore

The green sandy fields behind the beach at
Cill Mhuirbhí (Kilmurvey) are part of a machair
landscape. This forms when dune systems
are eroded down to the water table by a
combination of strong winds and heavy
grazing. Machair is found only in the west
of Ireland and the northwest of Scotland.

AD 2000

1000 BC

In Bronze Age times, the people who lived in Dún Aonghasa may have looked down on a wide
stretch of rocky foreshore rimmed by extensive sand dunes and possibly backing on to a lagoon
and some marshland.

Because the network of field walls had yet to be built, the higher terraces would have been covered
in rock scree. Stands of oak, ash, birch, alder, hazel, willow/poplar and pine probably grew wherever
there was adequate soil and shelter - the inland cliff behind the Visitor Centre would have been an
ideal spot.

Timber for building, fuel for burning

There are no bogs on the islands; trees too are very scarce. How did the early inhabitants manage for building materials and fuel? The excavations at Dún Aonghasa and Dún Eoghanachta produced burnt wood in the form of charcoal, most of it associated with domestic hearths. A wide range of trees and shrubs were identified: oak, pine, hazel and blackthorn were the most common but also present were willow/poplar, juniper, birch, ash, yew and holly.

A much fuller picture of the islands' vegetation history comes from scientific investigations carried out at An Loch Mór (The Big Lake) in 1996. The lake was cored at its deepest point and found to have a thick build-up of muddy sediments on the bottom. Analysis of pollen trapped in the samples provides a good picture of long-term vegetation and land-use changes for the islands during the last 10,000 years or so.

An Loch Mór, at the eastern end of Inis Oírr, is the largest lake on the Aran Islands.

These diagrams, based on data from Loch Mór, show a comparative representation of different types of vegetation cover (K. Molloy and M. O'Connell).

Trees Ferns Heath Tall shrubs Grassland Arable/disturbed

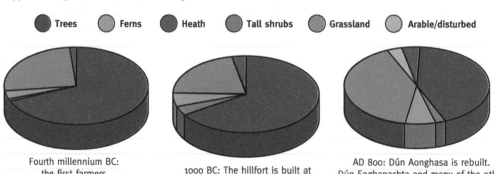

Fourth millennium BC:
the first farmers

1000 BC: The hillfort is built at Dún Aonghasa

AD 800: Dún Aonghasa is rebuilt. Dún Eoghanachta and many of the other Aran stone forts are built

Most of the walled fields on the islands were created in historic times. In the nineteenth century, in particular, an expanding population meant there was increasing demand for tillage to grow potatoes. Earlier inhabitants would have farmed a more open landscape, probably enclosing land only where crops had to be protected from livestock.

Threatened fuel shortages - Colmcille warns Éanna

The present almost treeless aspect of the Aran Islands may not have come about until the late 18th century, but a conversation between two saints, Éanna and Colmcille, in Beatha Colaim Chille (Life of Colmcille), written by Maghnus Ó Domhnaill in 1532, shows that lack of fuel was a concern well before that.

In response to Éanna's unwillingness to give a portion of Aran to him, Colmcille recites a litany of benefits that the islanders will miss out on. These include *'sufficient turf for making a fire'*. Ó Domhnaill notes that Colmcille's prophesy has proved true, as the people of Aran have *'neither turf nor fire-wood and must make fires with sun-dried cow-dung'*.

The Outer Enclosure wall

The road up to the fort leads to a modern gap in the outer wall. The outer wall was probably never much more than a metre or a metre and a half in height but it was cleverly built along the edge of a terraced drop. To anyone approaching the fort the wall appeared far more formidable than it actually was.

Tour Starts Here!

Parts of the wall look quite dilapidated and tumbled, but the section extending to the cliff (on your left as you enter the fort) is the best preserved stretch of the Late Bronze Age hillfort defences visible today. The wall was probably built around 1000 BC.

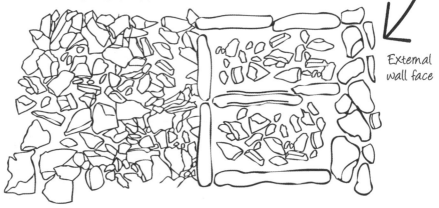

Bank of rubble

External wall face

Excavations in 1993 showed the wall was of unusual 'box' construction. Large edge-set flagstones were used to hold rubble fill; a bank of rubble was then piled against the inner wall face. The outer wall face was built in the usual way with stones laid down in rough courses. The box-like construction stabilised the wall and helped stop it collapsing down slope.

The original lintelled door pictured during excavations in 1992.

The original entrance to the outer enclosure lies slightly higher up the hill than the modern entrance - from the avenue you can see it away to the right. In the background, the mountains known as the Twelve Bens are usually visible across the sea in Connemara.

The Outer Enclosure

The outer enclosure is very exposed to Atlantic weather systems; most of it is broken sloping ground with little or no soil cover. While stock could have been corralled here, the primary reason for enclosing such a relatively large space may have been to physically segregate the hillfort from the surrounding farm landscape.

The ground plan of the hillfort consists of three enclosures nested one inside the other.

To get to the innermost part, you had to move onwards and upwards through a series of entrances.

For many Late Bronze Age islanders the outer enclosure may well have been as far as they got on most occasions.

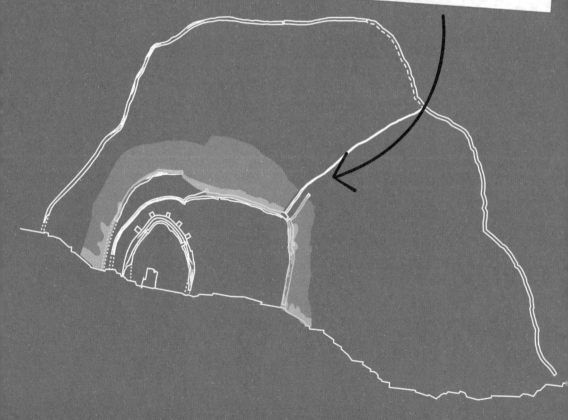

Processional space

Processional space is a feature of the sacred and public architecture of many cultures. Horizontal progress may be filtered through courtyards, vestibules, lobbies, atriums, doorways etc. There is also a vertical hierarchy of space (the 'upstairs downstairs' of a later period) with ramps, steps and stairs acting as controls.

At Dún Aonghasa access to the inner/upper areas may have depended on one's ancestry, status, rank, gender or age. At the top of the social hierarchy would have been the leading family or group of families who probably lived in the fort. Others who were held in high regard - religious leaders, poets who could recite the genealogy of the kin group, shamans and healers, elders, distinguished warriors etc.- may also have had access to all areas.

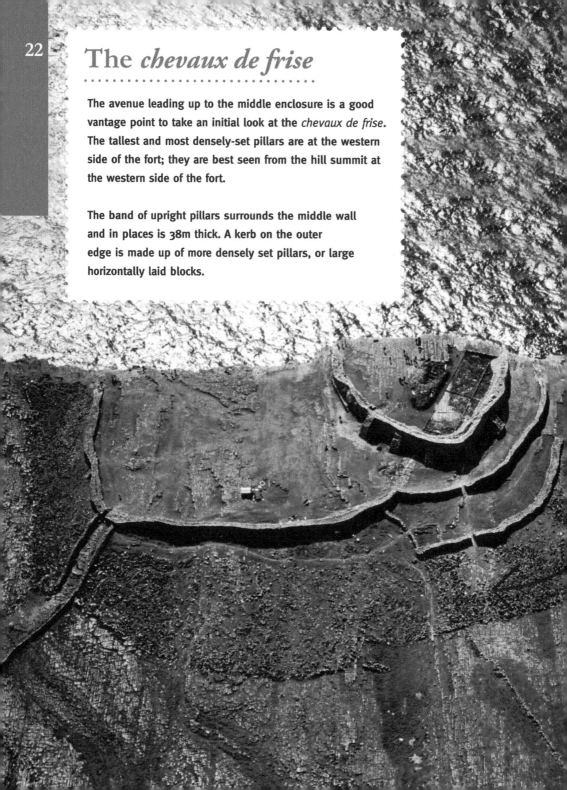

The *chevaux de frise*

The avenue leading up to the middle enclosure is a good vantage point to take an initial look at the *chevaux de frise*. The tallest and most densely-set pillars are at the western side of the fort; they are best seen from the hill summit at the western side of the fort.

The band of upright pillars surrounds the middle wall and in places is 38m thick. A kerb on the outer edge is made up of more densely set pillars, or large horizontally laid blocks.

A stone army

Some of the pillars are 2 metres tall and many weigh over half a ton. The stones were probably quarried on the spot and swivelled into position; they were held upright by being wedged against rock faces or rubble.

Chevaux de frise...campo friso...cavalos de frisa
(Friesian horses: a term borrowed from a device used to stop cavalry in medieval times.)

Gráin chatha (Gaeilge/Irish) *(appearance of battle)*

Piedras hincadas (Spanish) *Pedres clavades/dretes* (Catalan)

Pedras fincadas (Portuguese) *Pierres plantées* (French)*(standing or set stones)*

Chevaux de frise in Europe

Around a hundred or so forts with
a *chevaux de frise* have been
recorded in western Europe;
80% of these are located in the
mountainous north-western part
of the Iberian Peninsula.
Four Irish forts - including
Dún Aonghasa and Dúchathair
on Inis Mór - are known to have
used the device.

*The Dún Aonghasa chevaux de frise
is the most impressive example of this
type of barrier known to exist.*

● *Fort with chevaux de frise*

How old is the *chevaux de frise* at Dún Aonghasa?

The excavations did not provide a definitive answer to that question. Outside Ireland
excavated *chevaux de frise* can be bracketed into the period eight to second century BC.
Although there are no definitive dates for any of the Irish examples, at this point in time,
it seems that they belong to a much later era. At Dún Aonghasa, the erection of the
chevaux de frise may have been the final 'improvement' made by the Early Medieval builders.

Military considerations

- A cordon of densely set, sharp pillars forms a very effective barrier; even today it is very difficult to get through the best-preserved zones of pillars.

- A *chevaux de frise* added defence in depth and in many ways performed the same function as a ditch. It slowed down the approach of oncoming attackers and acted as a trap for those retreating.

30 metres was the ideal range for throwing hand missiles with precision.

A symbol of wealth and power

- The construction of the *chevaux de frise* involved a huge investment of human labour. Being able to call on such a large labour force testified to the power of the king and the number of clients he could command, directly and indirectly.

- There were seven strong forts on the Aran Islands in Early Medieval times. We don't know if the aristocratic owners belonged to the same kin group, or shared a common overlord, but, when it came to the limited resources of the islands, they would have seen themselves as being in direct competition.

- We are all adept at reading symbols and it was no different in the past. The spectacular *chevaux de frise* tells a story of power, authority, command of resources and the leadership skills of perhaps one individual ruler to persuade the kin group to invest heavily in their future.

The Middle Enclosure

The middle enclosure is a created space, bounded along three sides by high walls. The hulking presence of the inner enclosure provides shelter from the south-westerly winds; the southern aspect means it gets the best of the available sunshine. Quarrying has made the enclosure reasonably level, although certainly not flat, and the eye is immediately drawn to the maritime vista.

Room To Improve

The Early Medieval builders retained the general plan of the Bronze Age hillfort, but they massively strengthened the original inner and middle walls and added two new walls on the western side.

On the middle wall the extra bulk was added to the inner side - the whole wall was then heightened and terraced. As a result of the later works, the Late Bronze Age wall is now largely obscured from view.

Profile of Middle Wall

Middle Enclosure

Outer Enclosure

Habitation layers built up during Bronze Age

⬤ Early Medieval Wall   ⬤ Bronze Age Wall

Outer Enclosure

Middle Enclosure

Inner Enclosure

Cliff Edge

Outer Enclosure

Chevaux de Frise

Modern Entrance

North Door

Middle Enclosure

Inner Enclosure

Cliff Edge

Late Bronze Age

The Late Bronze Age walls were 2 metres thick and probably around the same in height.

Early Medieval Period

The Early Medieval builders strengthened the original inner and middle walls. The middle wall is about twice the dimensions of the Bronze Age wall.

The North Door during excavations in 1995

The original entrance to the middle enclosure lay in the northern part of the wall (on the right as you enter the enclosure). There was an opening here in prehistoric times but the fine roofed doorway that survives probably belongs to the Early Medieval phase.

The North Door

A paved path led up to the door on the inner side and anyone coming or going had to cross three stone thresholds. From a security perspective this would certainly slow up progress. The idea of three thresholds - and possibly passing through three doors - may also have had some symbolic significance.

Rock steps at the 'new' door

The door is blocked up now because the outer lintel has cracked

The new entrance (the modern access point) involved an element of display - the stepped avenue outside it certainly makes for a dramatic approach.

The new entrance was orientated towards the north coast. By the Early Medieval period there would have been much more traffic in the bay below; there was also a monastery at the foot of the hill (near the Visitor Centre), probably on lands endowed by the fort owners.

The Inner Wall

The massive inner wall averages around 5m wide and is almost 6m high in parts. The Early Medieval builders added to both the inner and outer sides of the Bronze Age wall. As a result, the 2m wide prehistoric wall is now more or less completely enveloped and hidden from view.

The doorway to the inner enclosure was repaired in the nineteenth century, by which time most of the roof slabs had moved out of place. There would have been a wooden door, probably situated roughly where the modern gate is fitted, but no traces of any hanging or closing features are evident now.

The Inner Door

Strengths and Weaknesses

With regular maintenance, a drystone wall can survive for a millennium or more. There were some inherent weaknesses in the inner wall at Dún Aonghasa, however.

The front facade around the entrance seems to have been structurally weak from the outset - it is possible that a whole outer layer of facing collapsed here at some stage, leaving a much rougher 'inner facing' exposed. It is difficult to unravel the different phases of repairs but many hands certainly make for uneven stonework. The biggest programme of 'modern' repairs to the fort took place in 1884-1885.

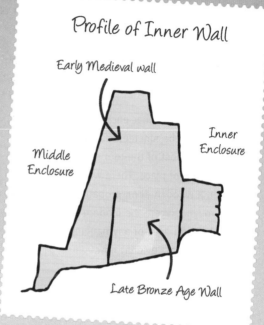

Profile of Inner Wall

Early Medieval wall

Middle Enclosure

Inner Enclosure

Late Bronze Age Wall

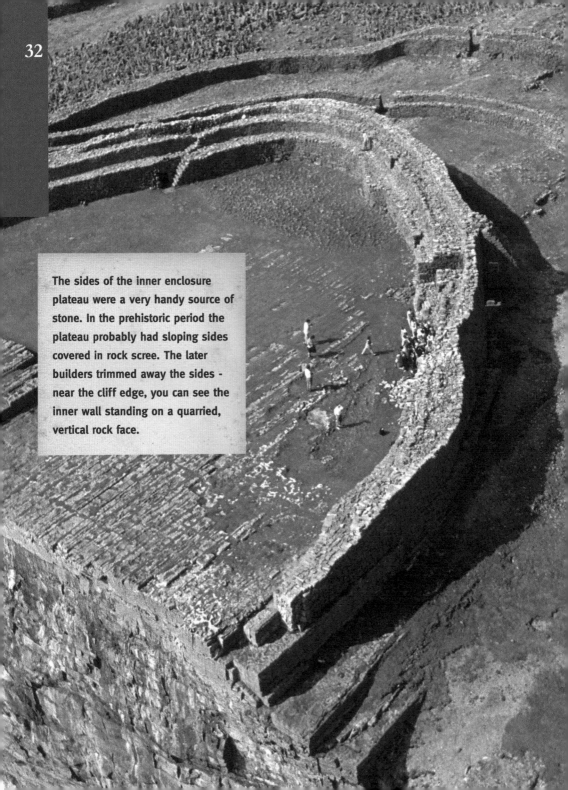

The sides of the inner enclosure plateau were a very handy source of stone. In the prehistoric period the plateau probably had sloping sides covered in rock scree. The later builders trimmed away the sides - near the cliff edge, you can see the inner wall standing on a quarried, vertical rock face.

Building the Walls

A drystone wall is built without any mortar or cement. The finish depends on the skills of the mason but perhaps even more so on the quality of the available stone. The fine regular-sided blocks that could be quarried on the hilltop make for a smooth even finish. Further down slope, the limestone becomes more craggy and consequently the finish of the outer wall - and even the outer face of the middle wall - is much rougher.

Late Bronze Age builder levering stone from hilltop

Quarrying the Stone

The most labour-intensive part of the whole enterprise was quarrying the stone. Ridges of rock (clints) separated by intervening hollows (grykes) make the carboniferous limestone on the hilltop ideal for quarrying. The limestone is also laid down in horizontal beds so that blocks can be wedged off with relative ease. The Late Bronze Age builders may have used a fire-hardened timber pole for the job; in Early Medieval times a pole tipped with iron may have been more common.

Once quarried, the stone had to be graded and sorted - the size of the facing stones decreased with height. The quarrying also produced tons of rubble and chippings and this was used for the wall core.

Around 1270m³ of stone was used to build the inner wall alone.

That calculation is based on the formula:

Volume of wall = 2.76m (mean height) x 549m² (area of base) with a 20% reduction for voids (spaces between the stones).

The batter or slope on the external wall face and the terraces on the interior reduced the overall quantity by around 30%.

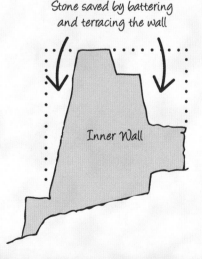

Stone saved by battering and terracing the wall

Inner Wall

Strengthening the Inner Wall

Strengthening the inner enclosure wall was not a very straightforward task. The Late Bronze Age wall hugged the edge of the upper plateau - outside was a drop that ranged from 1-2m in height. In order to carry the new foundations down over very uneven ground, the later builders first trimmed the plateau sides into a series of stepped ledges. Vertical layers of walling were then added to the original wall, each successive layer being independently faced and stepped further down the side of the plateau.

As well as making the wall more stable and less prone to large-scale collapse, the method made the logistics of building much easier and reduced the need for ladders and scaffolding. The first metre or so of the wall probably went up fairly rapidly. Above head height, the process was much slower as individual blocks and baskets of rubble had to be passed up to the masons either manually or by pulley.

TITLE: Late Bronze Age Builder

TRADE: Gobban

DATE: 1000 BC

**COMMUNITY PROJECTS
BUILDING A BETTER FUTURE.**

Sunrise	Barley Bread	Sunset
Sunrise	Limpets	Sunset
Sunrise	Barley Bread	Sunset
Sunrise	Limpets	Sunset
Sunrise	Boiled Bream	Sunset
Sunrise	Barley Bread	Sunset

TITLE: Early Medieval Builder

TRADE: Cronan

DATE: AD 800

**THE HIGHER THE WALL
THE SMALLER THE ENEMIES.**

Sunrise	Rye Bread	Sunset
Sunrise	Wrasse	Sunset
Sunrise	Rye Bread	Sunset
Sunrise	Wrasse	Sunset
Sunrise	Rye Bread	Sunset
Sunrise	Liver	Sunset

A close up of the wall fabric shows the contrast between the original stonework *(bottom half)* and the repairs carried out in the nineteenth/twentieth century *(top half)*.

The Repairwork

The masonry of the upper half is much more open. Smaller blocks have been chosen and the builders did not use spalls (small filler stones). They also clearly wanted to expose the smoothest face of the stones.

The coursing is very uneven - not breaking the joints has had a big impact here and vertical columns of masonry are subsiding unevenly. Viewed in profile, the curve of the wall face is much flatter on the repaired section.

◯ Late Bronze Age

◯ Early Medieval

◯ 19th – 20th century repairwork

Masonry of different periods on the exterior of the north door.

The Original Masonry

The best blocks were kept for the outer facades of the walls (first impressions count!). The stone is well-graded. Larger blocks laid horizontally (stretchers) are used for the foundations. Above this level, facing stones are generally laid as headers, i.e. the long axis of the stone runs into the thickness of the wall to create a better bond. Many of the headers are well over 50cms in length and weigh upwards of a quarter of a ton. The blocks are laid in rough courses; small wedges of stone are used to help even up the courses and to plug gaps.

Each stone was selected individually for best fit but, unlike later wall styles, the masons paid very little attention to breaking the joints - thus, rather than being staggered, 'ends' often align vertically. Cracks and imperfections are left on view. Over time, the fabric of the wall becomes tighter; the lack of bonding material means it can adjust well to the different settling rates of the wall face and the much looser core.

1870's

2010

Excursions to the Aran Islands were popular in the late nineteenth and early twentieth century and, with the advent of photography, Dún Aonghasa became a favourite destination for early camera enthusiasts.

Dunraven

The superb black and white photograph taken by the third Earl of Dunraven provided a vital clue as to the make-up of the inner wall. Dunraven photographed the northwest corner of the wall (to the right of the entrance) around 1870, fifteen years before the monument was repaired. A large V-shaped breach is visible where part of the external facade has fallen. His photograph clearly showed a second wall face behind the collapsed outer face - the first time this had been recorded on film.

The pioneer photographer Jane Shackleton at Dún Aonghasa in the early 20th century.

The wall was structurally weak at that point mainly because it had to curve at an angle across the jointing plane of the bedrock. The 'medial face' technique of building meant that only the outer skin of walling collapsed, leaving the rest of the wall intact.

In certain light (the later in the day the better) the outline of the repaired V-shaped breach can still be clearly made out. To prevent any further slippage, the stone buttresses were added after the 1880's repairs were completed.

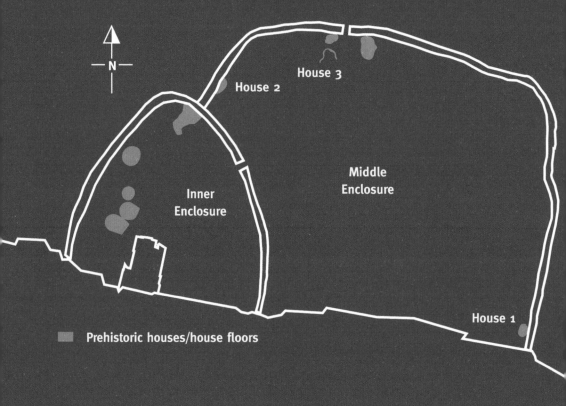

Prehistoric houses/house floors

Living in the Middle Enclosure

People lived in both the inner and middle enclosures generally tucking their houses in under the shelter of the walls. With an area of 5000 square metres, the middle enclosure could have accommodated a large number of houses, but during the 1992-1995 excavations, buildings were found at only three locations:

- House 1: Near the cliff edge on the southeast

- House 2: On the narrow strip of high ground between the inner and middle walls
  (in prehistory the middle wall curved across that space and joined up with the inner wall)

- House 3: Beside the original entrance to the enclosure on the north

Prehistoric Houses

The houses excavated in the middle enclosure belonged to the early history of the site. They were very poorly preserved - in most cases, all that remained were a few set stones where timber posts might have rested, or stone flags that had been part of a pathway or an internal floor.

House 1

A stretch of foundation walling was all that remained of this prehistoric house. It stood in a quarried hollow near the present cliff edge. Beside it was a midden (refuse mound) made up mainly of seashells.

House 2

The best preserved Late Bronze Age house in the middle enclosure stood on the high ground at the northwest corner. It was butted against the (now removed) stretch of the middle wall and measured 3m in diameter.

The walls were made of large slabs of stone set into midden refuse or wedged against steps in the bedrock. The east wall was missing - the entrance was probably located there. Radiocarbon dates from animal bone samples showed the house was built around 700 BC.

The residents disposed of their rubbish immediately outside the house. A very corroded and broken bronze axehead was found here - the only bronze tool found outside the inner enclosure.

House 2

Possible reconstructions of House 2. A rounded 'basket' form (above)
would give the wind less purchase than a conventional 'wall and roof' model (below)

What did the Bronze Age houses look like?

With so little structural evidence it's hard to say what the prehistoric buildings might have looked like originally. The likelihood is that the superstructures were of wood, made up either of upright posts or of lighter, bent timbers. External walls may have been made of sods, or wattle covered with plaster. Vegetation such as straw, reeds, dried seaweed, animal skins, felted wool or sods could all have been used at various times as roofing material.

This excavation trench lay just outside the *chevaux de frise* in the northern part of the fort. In the recent past, the paste-like daub was put to many uses on the islands - including as a plaster for internal walls.

Yellow daub lies between a layer of natural gravels and bedrock.

Prehistoric people spent comparatively little time indoors - conditions in the Dún Aonghasa houses would have been fairly cramped and much of the space must have been taken up by bedding.

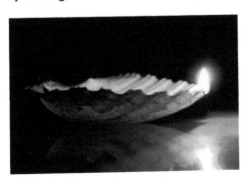

An open door or a central fire were probably the main sources of light. A few complete scallop shells found during the excavations may be the remains of lamps - a wick dipped in fish or whale oil held in a scallop shell was a common form of lamp in later times.

House 3

A Foundation trench cut into gravel.

B One of the post holes; the posts were wedged into position with stones.

C Bedrock - this part of the house was missing, probably because the posts rested directly on bedrock.

D A pit that contained a scallop shell.

E Gully, possibly for drainage.

An Unusual Building

A series of structures was found on the sheltered ground beside the North Door - some of these buildings may only have been in use while the hillfort was being built. The attraction of this particular spot was probably the presence of a thick deposit of gravel - up to 1m thick in places. This was the only part of the hilltop where a post-built structure could be clearly identified during the excavations.

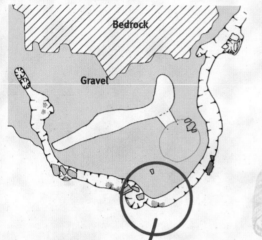

The ground plan defined by the postholes was very irregular (and incomplete) but the building seems to have had curved rather than straight walls and measured 4m in diameter. The door was in the west wall - an untypical location, as down to very recent times, doorways generally faced east, away from the prevailing wind.

A most unusual aspect of the building was that three or four handfuls of periwinkles had been deliberately and carefully trailed along the bottom of the freshly-dug foundation trench, and single scallop shells had been placed in two of the larger post-holes.

In the past, talismanic objects were frequently placed under the foundations, thresholds or hearths of houses in order to enhance the fortunes of the owners. Given the importance of the sea in the economic life of the Aran islanders, it is not surprising to find shellfish used symbolically for that purpose. Until very recently limpet shells were placed in the four corners of island houses on 1 February (formerly Imbolg, now St Brigid's Day) to ensure plenty for the year ahead.

Charcoal from one of the post-holes provided a sample for radiocarbon dating; it seems the building was constructed in the prehistoric Iron Age, probably sometime between 350 BC and 1 BC. It is not clear if it was a domestic house or had some other purpose - no floor or occupation layers survived. The location, immediately inside the North Door, could mean the building was linked to rituals associated with entering or leaving the fort.

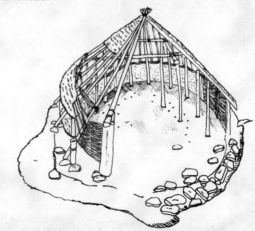

Brothers in Arms

One of the surprises of the 1992-1995 excavations was the discovery of a burial lying in a crouched position against the inner threshold of the North Door. The burial was originally covered with stone slabs but these had been moved at some stage. As found, the skull was missing but scattered teeth show that the body was complete when interred. The remains were those of a youth, aged between 14 and 16 years; there were no indications as to how he had died. A few bones of a second youth of similar age were also present in the grave. It is not clear if remains of the second individual had been removed to make way for a 'new' interment or if they had been robbed at a later stage.

Samples of bone from each individual produced broadly similar radiocarbon date ranges indicating that both youths had died during the last quarter of the first millennium AD (the full span is 680 - 950 cal. AD).

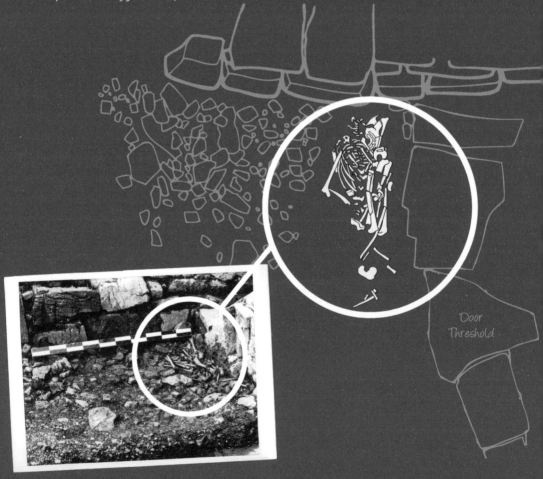

Door
Threshold

Path to Eternity

The crouched position of the body is unusual for the Early Medieval period - fully extended inhumation (as in modern burial) had been the norm for a considerable length of time. It may be that the family involved adhered to old ways and wanted their kin buried in the place and style of the ancestors. There may be more pragmatic reasons why this relatively narrow space was used. The stone-lined path leading up to the door looked like a ready-made grave and the gravel provided handy and easily-dug backfill.

Given that massive building works were in progress at the fort around the same time, it is not beyond the bounds of possibility that the youths died in a construction accident or accidents. There were many other potential 'killers' in Early Medieval Ireland, however, and many of the diseases that are treatable in modern medicine would have proved fatal at the time. A burst appendix, a tooth abscess, an infected wound could potentially shorten what was already a comparatively short life expectancy.

Group of Aran boys in traditional dress
photographed by Jane Shackleton in 1892

Head Hunters

Publication of Charles Darwin's 'On the Origin of the Species' in 1859 resulted in a flurry of scientific and popular interest in theories of evolution. The idea that physical attributes such as height, chest width, eye and hair colour and disposition of facial features etc. could be plotted on an evolutionary time line running from 'savage' to 'civilised' gained popularity.

Anthropometry in Aran.

In 1891, two eminent Trinity College scientists, Charles Browne and Alfred Haddon, arrived on the Aran Islands to assess the islanders position on the ladder of evolution. Regarded by some as descended from the mythical Fir Bolgs, the islanders were measured, assessed and graded for potential 'Firbolgery'. Women got less of a look in (presumably the scientists considered them to be further up the food chain!).

The results - and a detailed account of the landscape and way of life of the islanders - were published in 1893 in the *Proceedings of the Royal Irish Academy*, followed soon after by a series of similar studies on Connemara communities. In the event, the Aran Islanders got a good report, their keen vision and hearing, natural traits of honesty and generosity and robust moral fibre being singled out as especially praiseworthy.

On the Firbolg front, the conclusions were a bit more equivocal....

"To what race or races the Aranites belong we do not pretend to say, but it is pretty evident that they cannot be Firbolgs, if the latter are correctly described as small, dark-haired and swarthy".

Haddon and Browne 1893

During their time on the islands, Haddon and Browne visited some of the graveyards and let it be known that they were interested in 'old skulls' - could the missing skull from Dún Aonghasa have ended up in their collection?

The Inner Enclosure

······································

The inner enclosure is cupped like an ear to the Atlantic, which rolls on here uninterrupted for over 3000km - nearest landfall Newfoundland!

The terraces were essential for look-out purposes; stone steps made it easy to scale the wall quickly. Most of the stairs have been blocked up to help preserve the drystone walls.

Image based on a laser scan of the fort.

The Vista

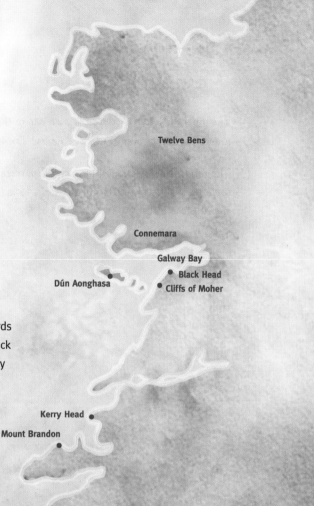

On clear days there is an unrestricted view down the west coast of Ireland as far south as Kerry Head. In exceptional conditions (generally in winter) Mount Brandon on the Dingle Peninsula, Co. Kerry, can be seen on the horizon 104km away to the south. Closer to home, silhouetted against the skyline on the Clare coast, are the well-known Cliffs of Moher.

Following the Clare coast northwards to the Burren, Ceann Bóirne or Black Head marks the entrance to Galway Bay. On the opposite side of the bay, is the broken coastline of Connemara.

Twelve Bens

Connemara

Galway Bay

Black Head

Dún Aonghasa

Cliffs of Moher

Kerry Head

Mount Brandon

Twelve Bens

Across the sea in Connemara, the distinctive profile of the mountains known as the Twelve Bens are visible most days.

To the East

On the east (to you left as you look to sea) the land falls to An Sunda Caoch (the Blind Sound), so called, because in poor weather, mariners have mistaken it for a passage through to Port Mhuirbhi (the beach) on the north coast. In the seventeenth century, a tidal wave passed right across the island at this point - the event was possibly associated with an earthquake that affected much of northern Europe in April 1640.

An Sunda Caoch

The cliffs continue to the west of the fort - about 2km away the stone fort of Dún Eoghanachta lies hidden among the limestone terraces. The high ground bordering the cliffs is traditionally used as winter pasturage for cattle - a reversal of the usual west of Ireland practise - scarcity of water up on the terraces means cattle must be moved to the lower pastures for the summer months.

Dún Aonghasa Excavations 1992-1995

This photograph taken in 1992 shows the archaeological excavations in progress - the whole of the western half of the inner enclosure was investigated. Given the thin soil cover, and the fact that the site is so exposed to the elements, the results were far richer than expected. The Late Bronze Age strata were well-preserved, but most of the later occupation levels - dating to the Early Medieval period - had been weathered away.

. . . .

From the intimate space of their airy auditorium, the hillfort dwellers could look out on the meeting of land, sea and sky.

What is the platform for?

Is it a stage from which sacrifices could be made to the truculent watery gods of the Bronze Age or simply a lump of extra hard limestone that was just too difficult to quarry with primitive tools?

The only eye-witness account of a section of the cliff falling away relates to a tragic incident in 1837, when a fisherman was 'precipitated into the sea' as the cliff gave way under him.

Four Bronze Rings

On the cliff edge near the platform, lying close together just as they had been buried over two and a half thousand years ago, lay four well-preserved, bronze rings, each around four centimetres in diameter. On closer inspection they could be identified as two pairs, one set decorated with concentric circles, the other plain.

The rings had hollow cores and lateral holes for stringing; projecting buffers protected the metal around the holes. They may have been worn with some form of centre piece - a similar ring found in Co. Sligo had a large amber bead at its centre.

Ritual Rings

'Buffered' bronze rings seem to be a uniquely Irish artefact-type and less than eighty are known to exist altogether. Smaller examples, like the Dún Aonghasa rings, could have been worn on the person - as part of a belt or neck-chain for example. A majority are much larger and heavier, however, and overall, it seems the most likely use was as decorative horse trappings - pairs of rings could have been attached to bridles, halters, breast bands etc.

In the Bronze Age, the horse may have been considered an exotic species, perhaps even a cult animal to be brought out only on ceremonial occasions, such as seasonal festivals.

A sun cult?

Some archaeologists argue for the existence of a solar cult across much of Europe during the Bronze Age. Daily life was conducted to the rhythm of the sun's passage across the sky. The annual solar cycle marked out the major turning points of the seasonal calendar.

Why bury the rings?

Pledging... Deliberately buried groups of bronze objects (known as hoards) are a feature of the Late Bronze Age and are very often associated with watery places, such as bogs or lakes. The traditional interpretation is that they were votive offerings made to appease or obtain favour from divine powers. A deterioration in climate followed by environmental pressure may have provided plenty of reason to look for divine intercession at the time.

...or Hedging In the Bronze Age, ownership of bronze goods, and every stage of the manufacturing process - particularly casting, but also mining, smelting and trading the ores - was controlled by aristocratic elites. Too much bronze in circulation devalued its worth. Hoarding possibly involved an element of regulation - taking some bronze out of circulation made the commodity scarcer, while promoting it as a medium through which mortals could converse with gods endorsed and enhanced

Wall Chambers

Wall chambers are quite rare but a sizeable proportion of Irish ringforts (Early Medieval farmsteads) had underground chambers and passages, their location probably known only to the fort dwellers. Access to the Dún Aonghasa chamber may have been from the interior of a building.

The semi-underground passage at Cahercommaun fort, in the Burren Co. Clare, exited through the fort wall and connected with a natural crevice running down the face of a steep ravine.

A wall chamber at Dúchathair (the Black Fort) could only be reached via a long, low passage that ran behind one of the houses.

The Chamber at Dún Aonghasa

Tucked in at the foot of a flight of stone steps on the west wall is a small chamber. There may have been an entrance here at some stage. In the Early Medieval period, the gap was probably used to bring in stone, quarried in the outer enclosure. When the building works were completed, the opening was blocked off from the exterior - this explains why the rear wall is so rough in appearance.

The chamber would have had a solid wooden door originally; the stone threshold it closed against survives. Its main function was probably as a strongroom for keeping precious items under lock and key; the cool dark conditions would also have been ideal for storing foodstuffs such as seed corn and dairy goods.

Radiocarbon dates from charcoal and animal bones found at the entrance indicate that the chamber was in use (and probably built) sometime during the period AD 650 - AD 890.

Living and dying on the edge of the ocean

The inner enclosure was the most densely occupied part of the fort during all periods of the site history. The western side - where there was maximum shelter from the prevailing winds - was the preferred location.

Prehistoric Houses

It is hard to say how many houses might have stood there at any one time - perhaps at the peak of the hillfort occupation (1000 - 800 BC) there may have been around six buildings.

House Wall

No full house plan of that era was preserved but the houses were broadly similar in form to the prehistoric houses in the middle enclosure. The low wall of this prehistoric house probably supported a timber superstructure. Only a small part of the western side of the house survived.

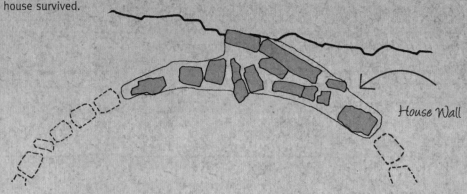

House Wall

Early Medieval Houses

The Early Medieval houses included a group of four very distinctive sunken-floor buildings. The most likely reason for this style of building was poor ground conditions - the soils in the inner enclosure are not only shallow, but very dry and loose. The closest parallels are houses found in Atlantic Scotland, often on sandhill sites.

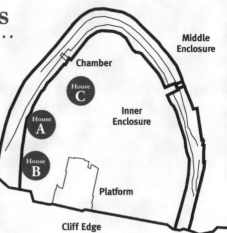

Middle Enclosure

Chamber

House C

Inner Enclosure

House A

House B

Platform

Cliff Edge

Most of the wall of this circular house survived. The entrance was in the east side - a large stone spanning the opening acted as both step and threshold; a hearth lay just off-centre in the interior.

There was no clue as to what the superstructures of the houses were made of. In House B, the gap between the foundations and the fort wall seems to have been only around 50cms. This would have been a very narrow interval for walls and a roof overhang. The inverted basket-type house might be a possibility here too.

House B

Neatly laid stones form the wall of the house.

The construction method was as follows:
• A circular pit, 5m in diameter and 50cm deep, was dug into the ground.
• The sides of the cut were neatly lined with upright stones.
• A paved floor was laid with the slabs being tightly wedged against the uprights.

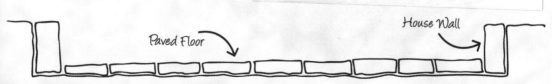

Paved Floor

House Wall

So long and thanks for all the fish

House C was of more robust build - very possibly this was the house associated with the wall chamber. It may also have been the last building to be occupied in the front. The house is a fairly typical example of the type of dwelling found in stone forts in the west of Ireland at the end of the first millennium AD. The roof may have been thatched with rye straw.

The interior of the house would have been divided up into a living/cooking space and a sleeping area. Bedding was usually made from dried vegetation such as hay or ferns, with animal skins or a woollen cloak providing heat.

House C

The full ground plan did not survive but the house seems to have been circular and around 5m in diameter. The doorway faced east and there may have been an annexe attached to the west wall.

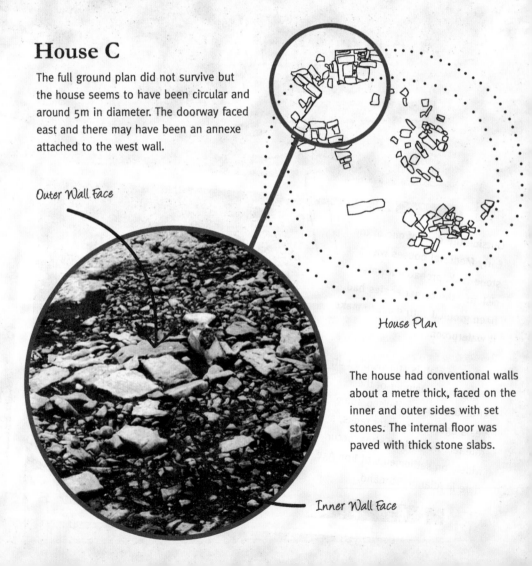

Outer Wall Face

House Plan

Inner Wall Face

The house had conventional walls about a metre thick, faced on the inner and outer sides with set stones. The internal floor was paved with thick stone slabs.

What House C may have looked like.

Outside the door of one of the Early Medieval houses was a stone tank, probably a water cistern - the corner angles had been grouted with daub to make it waterproof.

The base slab is still visible but, sadly, the remainder of the structure was vandalised some years ago. Stone water tanks, a rare feature on Irish sites, occur widely on settlements of Iron Age date in Atlantic Scotland.

Death

The life expectancy of prehistoric people was short - possibly only half that of the modern population. Infant mortality rates would have been particularly high - between scarcity of food, and childhood diseases, you were probably lucky to make it to adulthood at all.

Some of those born on the site did not have luck on their side - the remains of at least six very young infants were found during the excavations. Only parts of the skeletons survived in most cases. The complete burial shown on the left was carefully placed in a box-like rock cavity. The infant may have been still-born or died very soon after birth.

The radiocarbon date range for the burial (770–410 cal. BC) shows it belongs to the later part of the hillfort occupation.

Cremation was the usual burial rite in the Bronze Age but it may be that there was a separate rite for those who had not attained a certain age or status. This would not be unusual; there are many cultures/religions where different burial rites are used for very young children - in Hinduism for example, children under five are inhumed rather than cremated.

Infant grave

It's often hard to find traces of small children in the archaeological record but this spoon, made from bone or horn, could have been used for feeding infants.

The remains of an adult skeleton were found near the stone tank, but it is not possible to say for certain if the person was originally buried at that location. The only articulated part of the skeletal remains was the left upper limb, but part of a lower jaw and other widely scattered bones may be from the same individual.

Radiocarbon dating indicated that death took place in the prehistoric Iron Age, sometime between 170 cal. BC and cal. AD 60.

One item that could be associated with a burial of this period is a bronze fibula brooch found at the fort in the nineteenth century. Four of the nine other Irish brooches of this safety-pin type come from Co. Galway, all probably from burials.

Fibula Brooches were used as clothes fasteners and operated something like a modern safety pin. The Dún Aonghasa brooch is relatively plain. It must have been prized by its owner however, because it had been repaired at least once.

Bronze Fibula Brooch

Cremation remained the dominant burial rite in Ireland until the early centuries AD. Prehistoric Iron Age inhumations, found in the east of the country, are thought to be people with British connections, but there is also a much darker explanation as to why an individual might be buried as opposed to cremated...

Ritually killed individuals, or 'bog bodies' as they are generally known, are a phenomenon of late prehistory. It has been suggested that the Irish examples may be part of a wider practice of ritual deposition at significant boundaries, including the boundary between land and sea.

Is it possible that the Dún Aonghasa individual was ritually buried at the meeting place of land, sea and sky?

MENU

Monday
Barley mash & limpets.

Tuesday
Barley mash & periwinkles.

June 21st 860 BC

Nettle soup with wild garlic
Roasted limpets
Blood pudding with samphire
Roast lamb
Boiled bream
Guillemot eggs
Barley bread

Wednesday
Limpets & crab apples.

Thursday
Curds, dileasc broth.

Friday
Nothing to eat.

Sunday
Wrasse & barley bread.

Saturday
Barley porridge & blackberries.

MENU

September 22nd AD 800

Boiled periwinkles

Wrasse

Smoked guillemot

Liver

Rye bread

Blackberries

Fermented barley drink

Top Table AD 850

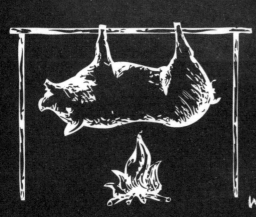

Pork

Salted fish

Sweetmeats

Honey

Cheese

Apples

Mead

Wheaten bread

Farming

Animal bones were reasonably well-preserved at Dún Aonghasa although a combination of thin soil cover, the hard rock surface and (yes!) tourist traffic meant they were in a very fragmented state. All parts of the carcases were present suggesting the animals had been killed and butchered on the site.

Late Bronze Age livestock

The graph shows the proportional representation of the main domesticated species (cattle, sheep and pig) in the food remains at Late Bronze Age Dún Aonghasa and a number of other well-known Irish prehistoric monuments (F. McCormick and E. Murray).

At Dún Aonghasa sheep are the dominant species - elsewhere cattle or pig predominate.

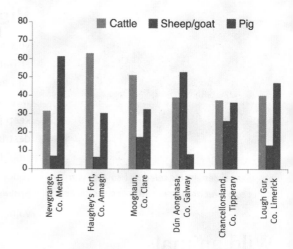

Cattle

On an individual basis, the meat yield from cattle was much higher. In an era when there was no way of preserving food, cattle may only have been slaughtered on special occasions.

Comparative size of Late Bronze Age cattle, pig and sheep.

Sheep

Sheep are a hardier species than cattle and are better able to weather spells of drought and limited supplies of winter fodder. The Bronze Age Aran sheep were similar in size to their contemporaries on the mainland but the island cattle were at the low end of the size scale.

There was evidence for a high rate of lamb and calf slaughter, lack of adequate foodstuffs to rear them probably being the main reason for the deliberate culling.

Soay sheep are regarded as being similar in size and appearance to prehistoric sheep.

Pig

Very few pig bones were found at Dún Aonghasa. Scarcity of nuts and acorns may have meant there was not enough foodstuff to keep pigs on the islands. The destructive rooting habit of pig would also have been a concern - once the sod was broken, the thin soils were vulnerable to wind erosion.

Boar tooth or tusk from the Late Bronze Age levels may have been worn as a trophy or a talisman.

Wild animals

The range of natural fauna is very limited on the islands; even some of our most common creatures such as frogs and foxes do not seem to have made it out there. Not surprisingly, then, wild animals do not feature much in the food remains from any period of the fort occupation.

Of non-domestic species grey seal possibly made the biggest contribution to the table. The few red deer bones present could have come from carcasses or cuts of meat brought in from the mainland. Part of a fox skull suggests a pelt, or, perhaps a trophy head was imported.

Wild carnivore skulls seem to have been regarded as cult objects along the Atlantic seaboard in prehistory. Fox, badger and deer skulls have been found carefully buried in pits and trenches; the most dramatic finding of all must be the head of a Barbary ape found at Navan Fort, Co. Armagh.

Livestock in the Early Medieval period

The Early Medieval animal bone assemblage was comparatively small at Dún Aonghasa. Fortunately, a much larger assemblage of this date was found during excavations at Dún Eoghanachta, a stone fort built around AD 800. Sheep also predominated there, followed by cattle.

Early Medieval stone fort located 2km west of Dún Aonghasa.

Pig was far better represented at Dún Eoghanachta, perhaps the fact that land enclosure was at a more advanced stage eased fears regarding soil erosion. Bulk feeds - such as boiled seaweed - may also have compensated for the lack of mast. In the Early Medieval period pork was one of the main foods served at royal feasts.

Arable farming

Conditions at Dún Aonghasa were not conducive to the survival of plant remains. The small number of charred cereal grains found tells us little about the agricultural practises of either the prehistoric or Early Medieval populations. Analysis of lake sediments from An Loch Mór on Inis Oírr helps to fill out the picture.

Cereals were an essential winter food. Barley was the main crop grown by the prehistoric island farmers, followed by oats. If wheat was grown at all, it may only have been in a few sheltered pockets. The Inis Oírr results highlighted the appearance of rye around AD 700. On the islands, rye was traditionally used for thatching as well as for cattle fodder.

Barley

Most of the identifiable cereal grains found at Dún Aonghasa were of six-row hulled barley, a fairly hardy variety that could be planted in winter or spring. Barley is a versatile food; it can be used whole in soups and stews, milled to make barley bread or ground into meal to make porridge.

Grinding stone from the Late Bronze Age levels. As well as grinding cereals, the stone could have been used to break down plants such as wild spinach, garlic and nettles.

Polydactyly

The thumb-like protrusions on the feet of this Bronze Age cow are duplicate toes, an abnormality known as polydactyly. The affected animal lived to maturity and butchery marks on the bones indicate that it was deliberately slaughtered and presumably eaten!

Polydactyly is an extremely rare finding in the archaeology record but quite common in modern Simmental and Holstein cattle.

Ballan wrasse, a bony but meaty fish.

Wrasse teeth from Dún Aonghasa. Wrasse are shellfish eaters and their strong teeth and jaws survive well on archaeology sites.

The Shore

The seashore, particularly the rocky inter-tidal area, was an important source of food for the fort dwellers. Fish, shellfish and edible seaweeds could be caught and collected there on a seasonal basis; edible vegetables grew in the splash zone. The occasional stranding of a large sea mammal was an extra bonus.

WOMEN PICKING LIMPETS   E. RIVERS

Fish

Wrasse and seabream (probably red seabream) were the most common varieties of fish eaten and together made up 97% of the total fish bone remains from the fort.

Both species are inshore fish and could be caught from the rocks or cliffs in summer and early autumn. Bream are now very scarce in the waters around the islands.

Seabream

Wrasse from the prehistoric levels at Dún Aonghasa measured 20-55cm in length; the largest specimens weighed around 3kg. The bream bones came from small and medium-sized fish, 25-40cm in length with a maximum weight of around 4kg.

Hand-line fishing for ballan wrasse from the cliffs at Dún Aonghasa in the early twentieth century.

The line was weighted with a holed stone and baited with crushed periwinkle or crab. It was then swung above the head and dropped 90m to the sea below. A rock shelf extends for about 50m offshore here with water depth being around 10 fathoms (60 feet).

Shellfish

· · · · · · · · · · · · · ·

The fort dwellers ate large quantities of shellfish. Limpets made up almost 80% of the shellfish remains with periwinkles forming most of the remainder. Both species can be collected at any time of year but, as limpets are nutritionally depleted in winter, the traditional harvesting season is from late Spring to Autumn.

> While a single meal of limpets provides only around 50 calories (compared to 100-300 calories for fish), shellfish were a rich source of minerals and vitamins and probably helped weather the leaner times of the year.

Limpets were usually roasted and a number of shallow pits in the bedrock seem to have been used for that purpose. Periwinkles were boiled; the snail-like meat could have been removed with a sliver of bone.

Seabirds

Seabirds and their eggs were a supplementary food for the fort dwellers. The birds were taken during the breeding season, in May and early June, when they would have been nesting on cliff ledges. Bird bones were far more plentiful in the Early Medieval middens. Guillemot was the main species eaten; the birds were probably split open and roasted.

Guillemot (foreground) and Cormorant.

A very unusual find in the Bronze Age levels was a bone of a Great Auk, a flightless bird now extinct. The stuffed bird shown above was rescued off the Waterford coast in 1834; it is believed to be the last Great Auk seen alive in Ireland.

Whale bone

Whalebone chopping board made by cutting off the projecting part of a whale vertebra like the one shown here.

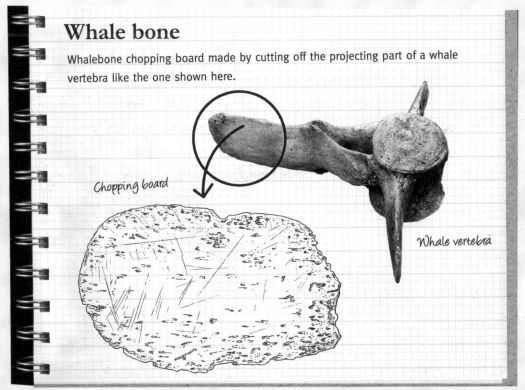

Chopping board

Whale vertebra

Life in the fort

The role of the fort, and the activities carried out in it, changed considerably between Bronze Age times and the Early Medieval period. Some of the material goods, particularly the items of personal adornment, also changed considerably while others show very little sign of development. The two eras are described here separately, beginning with the Late Bronze Age.

The Late Bronze Age hillfort

Between 1000 BC and 700 BC, people lived in the fort either continuously or intermittently. It is very likely these were the elite members of the Aran community, perhaps a leading family or group of families. It is hard to say what the population of the islands was at the time as, outside of the hillfort, no houses of Bronze Age date have so far been found. A rough estimate would be around three hundred people scattered across the three islands.

How long did it take to build the hillfort?

The Late Bronze Age hillfort encloses an area of almost 5 hectares (14 acres); each of the three walls was around 2m thick and 2m high. It probably took the whole community to build it - if you weren't actually on the job you were probably providing food for those who were. The following estimate takes account of time required to quarry and transport stone and is based on an average daily output of 1.5m³ of walling per person.

• If the work was carried out on a continuous basis, a workforce of around 100 people could have built the fort in under a year.

• If the task was carried out with a much smaller workforce, or one operating on a seasonal basis only, the time taken would increase accordingly - for example, 30 people working seasonally might complete the fort in around twelve years.

Why build a hillfort?

The hillfort was not simply a place of residence for elites. All the communal activities of the wider kin group probably took place there - religious ceremonies, seasonal celebrations, rites of passage, political planning, settlement of disputes, distribution of food surpluses, gift giving. The construction of the fort was a strong centralising force in the lives of the islanders and helped forge their identity as a distinct kin group.

The existence of the hillfort brought Late Bronze Age Aran society to the next level of social development, linking them with other communities at a similar stage of development. In an era when goods and raw materials could only be procured through exchange and gift-giving, status was very important. In a contemporary sense, we could see the hillfort as a vital piece of infrastructure that helped access a wider range of goods, essentials and luxuries.

Among those exotic goods were bronze objects and on at least one occasion the fort inhabitants made their own...

Bringing home the firewood - 914 BC

- CONOR McHALE -

Bronze casting - how it was done

Irish museums contain many hundreds of bronze tools, weapons and ornaments dating from the Bronze Age. Most were cast by skilled craftspeople using the clay mould method but evidence for manufacture is rare.

Dún Aonghasa produced one of the largest collections of Late Bronze Age clay moulds so far recorded in Ireland or Britain.

Specialist metal smiths were probably employed. A large hearth, set into sand at the northern end of the inner enclosure seems to have been the casting site. The sand may have supported and insulated the moulds during a pour. Longer moulds (e.g. those for swords) needed to be kept at an even temperature to ensure the molten metal did not solidify too quickly, and that air bubbles could escape.

Making the moulds

The face and obverse of an existing object or a wooden prototype are pressed into fine clay to make a double impression.

The two faces are matched up; the mould is wrapped in outer coarser layers of clay and carefully fired.

Bronze - in the form of ingots or recycled metal - is melted in a crucible and poured into an opening in the top of the mould. Complex hollow objects, like the bronze rings, required clay cores. When the metal has cooled the mould is smashed.

Cast objects are finished by removing any metal flashes, sanding down edges and polishing, if required. Stone, sand or pumice could be used as abrasives.

Types of object cast at Dún Aonghasa

The bronze objects cast at Dún Aonghasa included a sword, spearheads, knives, bracelets, pins and axes.

Axe mould

Type of axe cast

*Type of
spearhead cast*

*A possible match – bronze bracelet, probably for a child, and part
of a bracelet mould, both found during the excavations.*

Pumice

Around 150 pieces of brown volcanic pumice were found at the fort. As an abrasive, pumice may only have worked on soft materials, such as bone and leather, but it could have been used to burnish cast bronze items.

Pumice floats and the hillfort dwellers would have picked it up on the shore. Similar pumice from the west coast of Scotland has been geochemically correlated to eruptions from the Katla Volcanic System in Iceland.

Pumice

The community was largely self-sufficient growing, catching, collecting and processing their own food and making their own clothing, tools and weapons. Most activities were probably carried out in the open.

The finds from Dún Aonghasa

The large diagram shows the relative percentages of artefacts made from metal, clay, bone and stone; beads are included in a separate category. The smaller diagrams show the number of individual artefacts made from metal and clay.

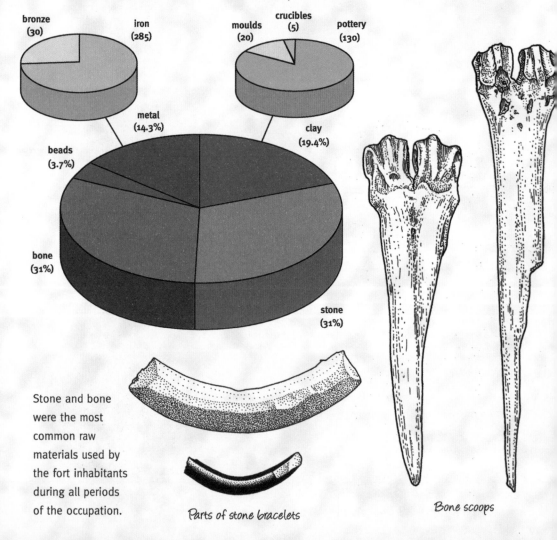

bronze (30)
iron (285)
moulds (20)
crucibles (5)
pottery (130)
metal (14.3%)
clay (19.4%)
beads (3.7%)
bone (31%)
stone (31%)

Stone and bone were the most common raw materials used by the fort inhabitants during all periods of the occupation.

Parts of stone bracelets

Bone scoops

Preparing and cooking food

The stone axe was the single most important implement of early farmers. By late prehistory large numbers of bronze axes were also in circulation among the better off. In addition to chopping down trees and carpentry work, axes could be used for killing and butchering animals.

Stone axe

One of three stone axes found during the excavations. It was made by modifying a cobble picked up either on the shore, or in clays weathered out from between the limestone beds.

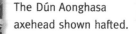

The Dún Aonghasa axehead shown hafted.

Knife/blade tip

Many of the animal bones found on site had chop and cut marks, possibly made by metal tools. Only the tip of this knife blade survived - it is twisted out of shape and may have been scrap destined for recycling.

Bone point

Bone points may have been used primarily to extract shellfish meat or bone marrow - over 100 were found on the site.

Shale axe

The fine lines may be due to grinding at the manufacture stage or wear when the axe was in use.

Pottery

The prehistoric pottery from Dún Aonghasa is of a type known as 'coarse cooking ware' - the fabric is very gritty and the vessels seem to have been used exclusively for cooking.

The pots were handmade and unglazed; the largest - around 30cm tall - resembled a modern planter in shape. Some had bevelled rims so they could take a lid. Pot covers - flat stone discs chipped around the edge for a good fit - were also found at the site.

Three fire-cracked stones found outside one of the prehistoric houses were probably used as pot stands for cooking. The stones had been laid flat side up and carefully levelled by placing smaller stones underneath.

A few pot sherds had burnt food residues attached. Scientific analysis was not conclusive, but foodstuffs of plant, animal and marine origin were all probably cooked in these vessels.

Some of the sherds had grass-marks on the walls, inside and out. It seems grass was pasted on to the wet clay once the vessel was shaped, possibly to help firing. Open firing in a bonfire was the usual method of pottery production in late prehistoric Ireland.

Roasting over an open fire would have been the most common method of cooking meat. Analysis of the charcoal remains in the domestic hearths indicated that people foraged for firewood, picking up whatever was available. For the bronze casting, however, only oak wood was used - oak is long burning and produces few sparks.

The number of bronze razors that survive from the Bronze Age suggests people - or perhaps just a certain sector of society - were clean-shaven. Well-preserved human remains from elsewhere in Europe show that Bronze Age people also tattooed their skin, but it is not known how widespread this practise might have been.

A bronze tweezers found at Dún Aonghasa was probably used for much the same purposes as a modern set.

People used costume to show their wealth and status and to highlight their role or rank in society. Woollen tunics and cloaks may have been worn mainly by the elite. For the less-well off, undyed clothing made from animal skins, or whatever coarse fibres were available, was probably the norm.

No remains of clothing were found at the site, but among the artefacts, were items that could have been used for cleaning animal hides, boring holes in leather, spinning wool and sewing textiles. The variety of clothes fasteners gives some indication of dress styles.

Woollen clothing

The coat of prehistoric sheep was hairy rather than woolly and was probably plucked rather than sheared.

The coarse brown and cream-coloured wool of Soay sheep is shown here with much finer white wool from a modern merino breed.

Bone spindle whorl made from the head of an animal femur.

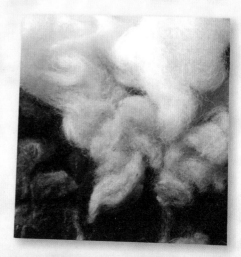

Wool was hand spun. A whorl threaded onto a drop spindle gave the necessary momentum to twist the fibres into yarn.

Bone needles

Almost 100 complete or fragmentary needles and pins were found during the excavations. All were made from animal bone and the presence of unfinished examples shows the manufacturing was done on site. The typical bone needle had an eye at one end.

These double-pointed needles have a central perforation and a slightly convex profile. They are an unusual type and may have been used for sewing coarse textiles or coiled fibres.

Processing animal skins and hides

Animal skins might be salted, beaten, rubbed with sand or some other abrasive before finally being oiled to keep them supple. Alternatively they could be de-haired and tanned to make leather.

These bone knives made from cattle ribs were probably used to scrape fat from animal hides.

Pounders and rubbing stones made from cobbles picked up on the shore formed a very large part of the Dún Aonghasa tool assemblage. They served a variety of purposes, from tool manufacture and the processing of raw materials, to food preparation and the fine finishing of items of dress.

Bróga urleathar (leather shoes), were worn by islanders down into the twentieth century but the simple form could have a very long history. The shoes were made from a single piece of cowhide worn hair side out and tied across the instep. The cowhide was salted and soaked in lime to remove the fats. The exceptionally fine pair shown above were for a child.

The polish on the tips of these finely made points suggests they were used as boring tools, possibly for making holes in animal hides.

Clothes fasteners

Pins

Bone pins seem to have been the most common type of clothes fastener used by the hillfort dwellers. The pins were not very robust, perhaps indicating they were for summer apparel. Most were plain with just a slight expansion at the head.

Some were perforated so that they could be secured with a string; a slight nick on the side of the stem kept the string from slipping off. A few had more elaborate nail-shaped or paddle-shaped heads.

The pinhead mould below seems to be for a small version of a sunflower pin, an ornament class that was very popular in northern Europe during the Bronze Age.

Pins with elaborate heads also feature in the clay mould assemblage. The ball-headed pin cast in the above mould would have looked like the dress pin (left) in the collection of the National Museum of Ireland.

Sunflower Pin
The reconstruction is based on a laser scan of the mould.

Beads

Amber beads

As an exotic import, amber (fossilised tree resin) was highly prized by Bronze Age elites. Its translucent 'liquid gold' appearance is very attractive - in later times the substance was considered to have magical healing properties.

Around a dozen, mostly large, amber beads were found in the inner enclosure. Some were badly burnt, their surfaces crazed and discoloured.

Most of the prehistoric amber found in Ireland came from the Baltic region, arriving via a series of trade interactions. The Dún Aonghasa beads may have been brought via a riverine network of traders working their way down the rivers and lakes of the north midlands. Alternatively, the islanders may have been part of a maritime trading network that linked the Atlantic islands of Ireland and Scotland with southern Scandinavia.

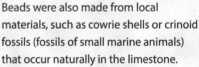

Beads were also made from local materials, such as cowrie shells or crinoid fossils (fossils of small marine animals) that occur naturally in the limestone.

Blue glass beads were popular from late prehistory down into Early Medieval times. This makes them difficult to date, but analysis of elements (copper, lead, cobalt etc.) Included in their make-up helps to place them along a time-line. Only one of the fourteen blue beads from Dún Aonghasa seems to belong to the Bronze Age - copper was the main colourant used for the small turquoise bead shown above.

The fossils were picked up in the soils - most are only a millimetre or two in size. In later times, fossils were often worn as charms.

Only half of this bead survived - it is made from a piece of brown pumice probably picked up on the shore. The only other pumice bead recorded in Ireland comes from a burial at Tara, Co. Meath.

The Prehistoric Iron Age

Compared to the Bronze Age and the Early Medieval period, traces of the prehistoric Iron Age population of Dún Aonghasa were few and far between. We know there were people present in the fort at stages between 500 BC and AD 500 - the partial remains of the adult burial and the fibula brooch belong to that period. Some of the other finds - plain bone pins and stone pounding tools for example - could belong to any phase of the site's history.

In the past, it was widely believed that the stone forts of the Aran Islands had all been constructed during the prehistoric Iron Age. That theory was based largely on the presence of *chevaux de frise* at two forts - Dún Aonghasa and Dúchathair - and on the fact that many drystone monuments in the Atlantic regions of Europe date to the Iron Age. The popular belief that the forts had been built by the mythical Firbolgs also kept the theory alive.

Dún Chonchúir, Inis Meáin

At the present time, there is no archaeological evidence to support a prehistoric Iron Age date for the building of the Aran forts. Like Dún Aonghasa, the bigger forts, such as Dún Chonchúir and Dúchathair, may have Bronze Age origins. All the monuments stand at prime points on the landscape and it would not be surprising to find that people lived at those locations during many periods of the past.

The findings from the excavations, and other research, suggest that the time when all seven Aran forts were in contemporary use, was between AD 800 and 1000.

The footprint left by Iron Age people, especially in the west of Ireland, seems to be exceptionally light. Wider use of perishable materials may provide part of the explanation. Iron itself does not survive the ravages of time as well as bronze; this is particularly true in coastal areas where salt-laden winds speed up corrosion.

The palaeoecological investigations at An Loch Mór give us an insight into what was happening on the islands during the Iron Age. The pollen record for AD 100-500 shows grasslands being overtaken by shrubby vegetation and invasive juniper scrub.

The investigating scientists, Karen Molloy and Michael O'Connell, suggest that farming declined to such a degree during this period, that grasslands more or less totally reverted to scrub and woodland, at least for a time. A similar decline in farming activity has been recorded more or less throughout the entire country - as a result, the early centuries AD period is often referred to as the 'Late Iron Age Lull'. In the case of the Aran Islands, it is not until around AD 500 that an upsurge in farming activity again registers strongly in the pollen record.

The photograph, taken in 1978, shows Colm Mór Faherty of Inis Meán making (and wearing) the traditional footwear of the islanders. Organic materials are perishable - only the buttons on the jacket might survive the ravages of time!

Perhaps the decline in farming activity signals some kind of population crisis, brought about by adverse climate, disease of animals or humans or a combination of all these factors. Even so, it seems the islands were not entirely deserted and those that remained had to live somewhere.

The Architecture of Power

Over the ages forts and fortifications have been a potent symbol of power across the globe, their presence and form communicating strong messages about the organisational structure of contemporary society.

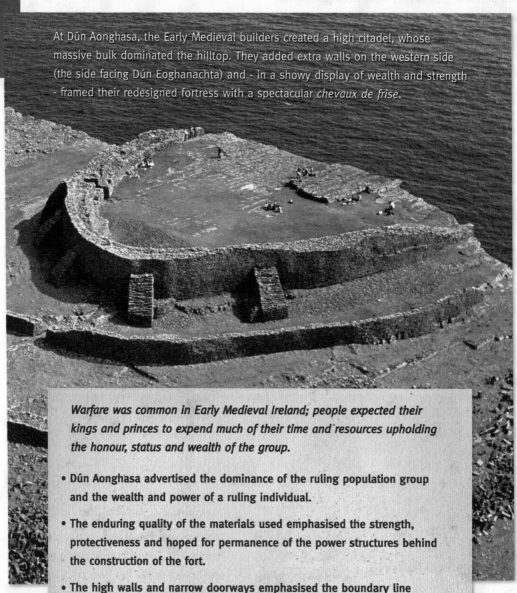

At Dún Aonghasa, the Early Medieval builders created a high citadel, whose massive bulk dominated the hilltop. They added extra walls on the western side (the side facing Dún Eoghanachta) and - in a showy display of wealth and strength - framed their redesigned fortress with a spectacular *chevaux de frise*.

Warfare was common in Early Medieval Ireland; people expected their kings and princes to expend much of their time and resources upholding the honour, status and wealth of the group.

- **Dún Aonghasa advertised the dominance of the ruling population group and the wealth and power of a ruling individual.**

- **The enduring quality of the materials used emphasised the strength, protectiveness and hoped for permanence of the power structures behind the construction of the fort.**

- **The high walls and narrow doorways emphasised the boundary line between the privileged insider and the excluded outsider.**

Early Medieval Dún Aonghasa

For the Early Medieval islanders, the strongest political links remained with Clare and the wider Munster region. Two principal groups may have been jostling for power locally - the Eoghanacht Ninussa, part of a federation of peoples whose over-king was seated at Cashel, and the Corcu Mruad, an indigenous people based in the Burren. Over time, as political power became more centralised and political boundaries more fixed, the position of the islands on the frontier between Munster and Connacht gave them added strategic interest.

By AD 800 a majority of Irish people were Christians. The Early Medieval church was wealthy, powerful and highly political - more often than not its bishops and abbots were drawn from the ruling lay dynasties. The founder of Aran's most famous monastery, the sixth century Éanna or Enda, was held in very high esteem as a holy man. His monastery attracted eminent ecclesiastics, many of whom were associated with powerful foundations and dynasties on the mainland.

Teampall Benán, a small church built around a thousand years ago as part of the monastery of Éanna or Enda.

The man commemorated on this stone 'Tomas Áp' (Thomas the abbot) was probably well-known to the fort dwellers. The stone can be found at na Seacht dTeampall (the Seven Churches), a monastery that lies about 2km west of Dún Aonghasa.

Dress and costume

Thanks to better preservation of items of clothing, and descriptions and illustrations in manuscripts, a good deal is known about Early Medieval costume. There was a far greater range of expensive fabrics and exotic dress ornaments available, and as a result the divide between aristocratic clothing, and the clothing of the labouring classes had widened. Other sectors of society - the church and the warrior class for example - wore distinctive costume and hair styles in order to proclaim their rank and livelihoods.

Comb from Dún Aonghasa, ninth/tenth century.

Double-sided bone combs with fine teeth were common among the wealthy and, as well as grooming, were used to control head lice. By the time this comb was in use, many aristocratic women wore a head veil. Aristocratic men were either clean-shaven or wore a beard and moustache; soldiers and lower-class men wore a long moustache without a beard.

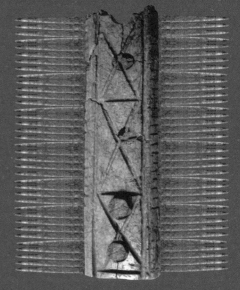

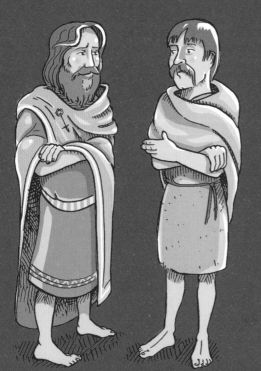

Léine: a sleeveless tunic that could be white or coloured, embroidered or plain. It was often tied at the waist by a belt; later versions had a large collar or hood.

Brat a rectangular cloth, wrapped like a shawl around the body. The size, material used and colour depended on the status of the owner.

The brat of a wealthy person was long enough to wrap five times around the body or to trail behind if one stood upright in a chariot.

Clothes fasteners

Clothes could be fastened with brooches or pins.

The head of a brooch-pin found at Dún Aonghasa in the early nineteenth century; a pin found during the 1992-1995 excavations may be the missing piece. The circular setting would have held a precious stone or stud - amber, rock crystal, glass and enamel were all popular embellishments at the time.

This bone pin had rolled down between the paving stones in one of the Early Medieval houses; it was probably worn with fine fabric, such as light wool or linen.

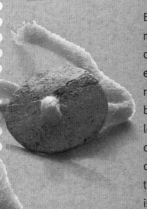

Even the colour of your clothes marked out your social status - only the wealthy could afford expensive dyes like blue woad and red madder. Woad was imported, but madder may have been grown locally. An eight century text outlining the taxes due to the king of Cashel from his subjects, refers to two taxes relating to the Aran islands - salanngabál (salt tax) and rodgabál (madder tax).

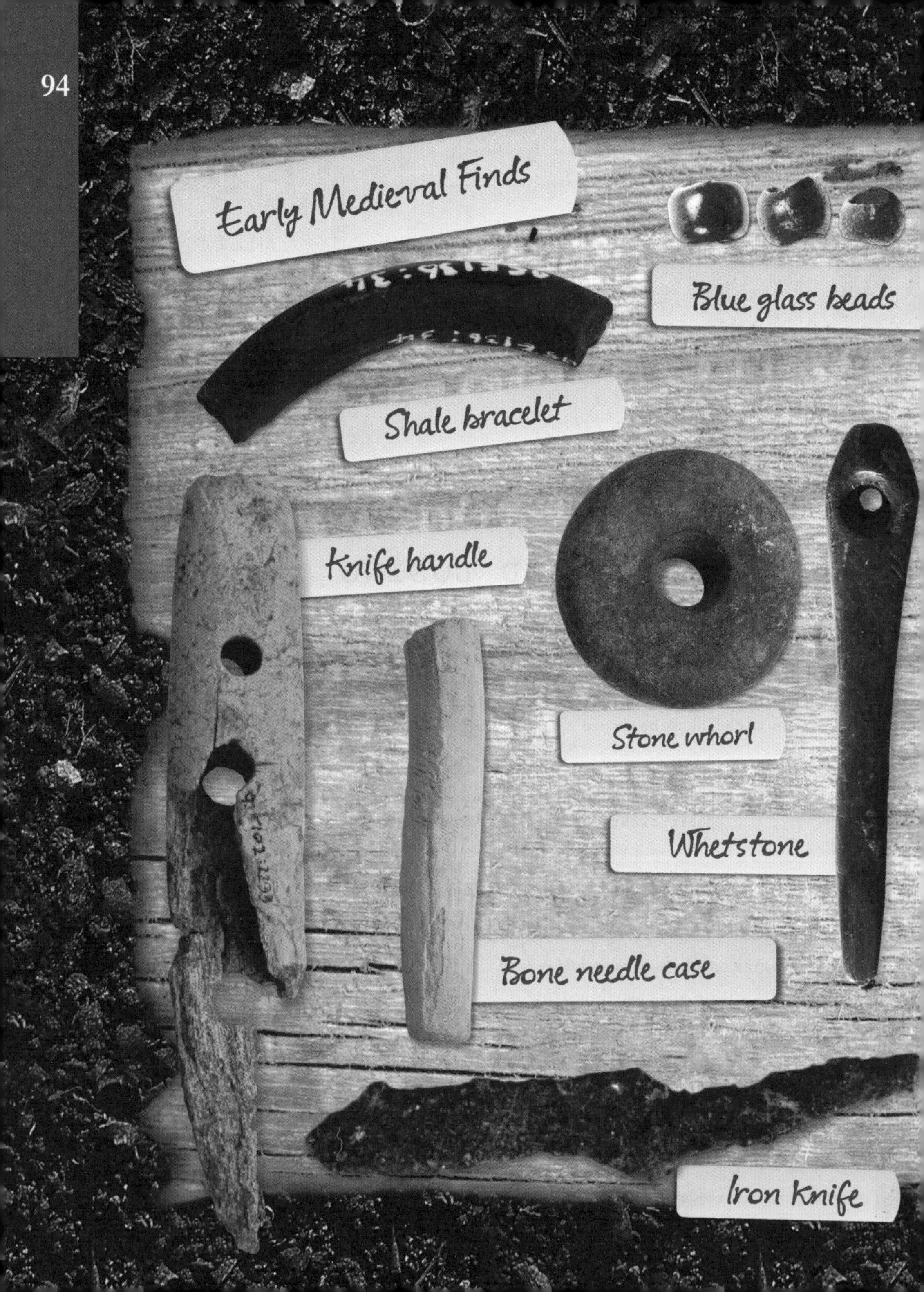

Early Medieval Finds

Blue glass beads

Shale bracelet

Knife handle

Stone whorl

Whetstone

Bone needle case

Iron knife

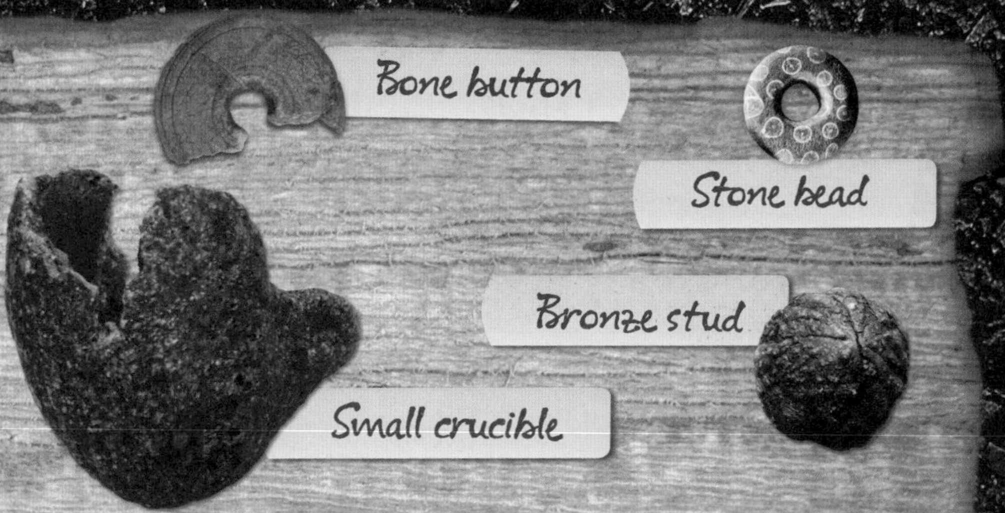

Bone button

Stone bead

Bronze stud

Small crucible

FINDING AND LOSING

Some of these objects were discarded, others were
accidentally lost and a few may have been deliberately
hidden for reasons we can only guess at now. Imagining can
be the best part of being an archaeologist...who these
things might have belonged to, a time when they were all
in use...

Perhaps a late summer's evening AD 850...
           ...their owners are sitting around a fire...

The boy wears a pendant bead made from a limestone pebble;
from his belt hangs a fine whetstone. His foster sister wears a necklace
of imported cobalt-blue beads and a shale bracelet. The women are
spinning - their stone whorls making a slight whooshing noise. The men
are whittling with iron knives - one man puts the finishing touches to a
bone needle case, another scores out circles on a bone button. A visiting
smith scrapes bronze spills from a small crucible - he hopes it will be
enough to repair the back of a bronze stud.

The life of children

In Early Medieval times it was common for the children of the well-off to be fostered out at a very young age - the practise helped create or cement alliances between leading families.

There were strict laws governing fosterage:

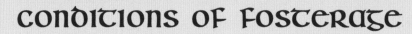

conditions of fosterage
aristocratic children

to wear cloth of a different colour every day
and multiple colours on sunday

to be given stirabout made from barley
wheat and new milk flavoured with
honey and second helpings if desired

curriculum to include (for boys)
horsemanship and chess-playing; (for girls)
embroidering and sewing

children of the lowest
fostered grade – the ochaire

to wear old clothes of black and
fawn and grey colour

to be fed limited rations of stirabout made
with oatmeal and buttermilk, flavoured
with a dab of salt butter

curriculum to include animal husbandry, grain
production, mastery of the quern and the spindle

Bonds between foster-children were strong - the tragic duel fought by two foster-brothers, Cú Chulainn and Ferdia, was one of the most popular tales in Early Medieval Ireland. It is part of the great heroic saga known as *Táin Bó Cúalnge* (The Cattle Raid of Cooley).

Perhaps a thousand years ago or so, a group of young fosterlings sat in the fort listening to the story of that fierce battle...

I CANNOT FIGHT YOU.

Images from: 'Celtic Warrior: The Legend of Cú Chulainn, © Will Sliney'

...clasped his two arms round him and carried him - weapons, armo

A din and a thunder, and a clatter and a clash, the shield-cry...th

Fer Diad's heart. Alas o noble warrior I thought th

Cú Chulainn struck him with h

washed and bathed, with hair plaited and beard shorn. He wears a dark purple mantle ar

Our famous foster-mother bound us in a blood pact of friendship Ó Cú Chulainn

a handful of water cress, a handful of laver, a

Have with you Ó Cú Chulainn, weapons harsh and hard and famed in song.

Fer Diad you have come to the gap of dange

If I am to go and fight with my foster brother, hard the task, great the disaster.

The storyteller's voice rises over the walls and out across the rocky fields where the
children tending the flocks of sheep, huddle close and dream of a world full of honey
and wheaten bread and clothes made from all the colours of the rainbow.

Misery has befallen us, Scáthach's two fosterlings - I broken and blood-red, your chariot standing empty

and harness - north across the ford. Alas o noble warrior Fer Diad...

...loved Fer Diad would live after me for ever. Yesterday a mountain-side, today nothing but a shade

...spear above the shield and it broke his ribs and pierced

...bed-striking of swords...and the deep voice of the battle-warrior

...handful of seaweed and after that a drink of cold sandy water.

...his hand he grasps a broad-headed spear, blood-stained, fiery, flaming

Sharp weapons will be wielded against you

Has the fort been restored?

Dún Aonghasa was made a National Monument in 1880. Shortly afterwards, under the newly set up 'Board of Works,' the Aran stone forts were among the first secular monuments in the country to undergo conservation work.

1884-5 Appendix to the 53rd report of the Commissioners of Public Works Ireland	
Works are in progress at the early churches and stone forts in the island of Arran	
North Arran Island	£308 · 9s · 11d
Inish Meáin	£76 · 11s · 5d
Jerpoint	£591 · 2s · 1d
Mellifont	£583 · 7s · 2d
Templemolaga	£16 · 13s · 10d

Repairs to Dún Aonghasa were carried out in 1884-85 and almost immediately proved controversial. In an era when picturesque ruins were popular aesthetic subjects, the transformation from 'chaotic heaps of stone' to neat even-topped walls did not prove popular. The restorers were accused of 'rebuilding' rather than 'conserving' and of inventing features that did not exist (or at least survive).

In 1857, a banquet in Dún Aonghasa was one of the highlights of an excursion to the islands by the British Association for the Advancement of Science. The outing was led by a notable antiquarian of the day - William Wilde, father of Oscar - who declared Dún Aonghasa to be 'the last standing place of the Firbolg aborigines of Ireland'.

Among the eminent antiquarians present were George Petrie (left) and John O'Donovan (right) – their descriptions of the fort dating from the 1820's and 1830's are the earliest detailed accounts on record.

Thomas J. Westropp

Thomas J. Westropp from Co. Clare is probably Ireland's greatest field archaeologist. At his own expense, and often travelling by horse and cart, he visited hundreds of archaeology sites in the west of Ireland between the 1880's and his death in 1922. His first visit to Dún Aonghasa was on a family outing in 1878, but he returned to sketch and photograph the fort on many occasions during the next forty years.

In 1910 Westropp published a very detailed article on the restoration of Dún Aonghasa, sifting through all the pre-restoration accounts and commenting on the repairs. He concluded that the restorers had not 'invented' features or been 'over-zealous' in their work.

So what was done in 1884-85?

- Major breaches in the walls were repaired.
- The terraces were repaired, quite extensively along some stretches.
- The inner door was repaired...and has been repaired again since.
- The buttresses on the exterior of the inner wall were added to prop up leaning masonry.
- The interior of the site was cleared of rubble.

Drystone work needs regular maintenance. Damage to the walls is an ongoing concern for the Office of Public Works, who maintain the fort. The closing off of access to the terraces has helped matters, and, with regular maintenance and visitor co-operation, the monument should be around for many generations to come.

Dún Aonghasa, collapsed inner wall in 1954

Has half of Dún Aonghasa fallen into the sea?

This is not an easy question to answer.

Relentless battering by wind and wave means there are cliff-falls all along this coast from time to time. In fact, the Atlantic facing coastline of the islands is littered with broken boulders, huge chunks of fallen cliff that the sea turns back against the land. Even in a fairly homogenous geological landscape like the Aran Islands, however, the rate of cliff recession is difficult to assess.

Where does this leave us?

- Most geologists agree, that, presently, it is impossible to offer any reliable estimate as to the extent of land loss on the islands in the past.

- The further back in time we go, however, the greater the possibility that there was significant additional land on the seaward side of the fort.

- It would have made no sense to butt a circular enclosure against the cliff-edge. When first built (around 1000 BC), the outer enclosure wall probably stopped at the cliff-edge but the middle and inner walls may have been fully curvilinear.

- Between the end of the Bronze Age (around 700 BC) and the rebuilding of the fort around AD 800, the likelihood is that a good chunk of the outer enclosure, and perhaps some of the middle enclosure had both disappeared. The original inner enclosure may have been still intact. We don't know if the Early Medieval builders strengthened the entire circuit of the wall - they may well have decided that there was no need for a substantial wall on the seaward side.

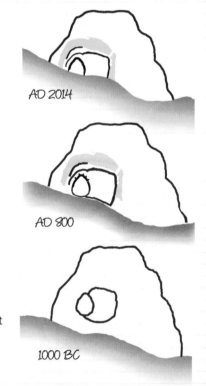

AD 2014

AD 800

1000 BC

Dún Aonghasa and Cahercommaun

Dún Aonghasa is often compared to another triple-walled Early Medieval fort - Cahercommaun in the Burren, Co. Clare. Cahercommaun stands at the edge of an inland cliff and we can be fairly certain that there has been little or no erosion since it was built around AD 800.

Cahercommaun, The Burren, Co. Clare.

The outer and middle walls terminate at the cliff-edge. The inner wall continues along the edge of the drop but is much slighter along that section (2m in width as opposed to 8m along most of the remainder of the circuit).

A slighter cliff-edge wall seems a very likely scenario at Dún Aonghasa also. The wall may only have disappeared after the fort was abandoned altogether around AD 1000.

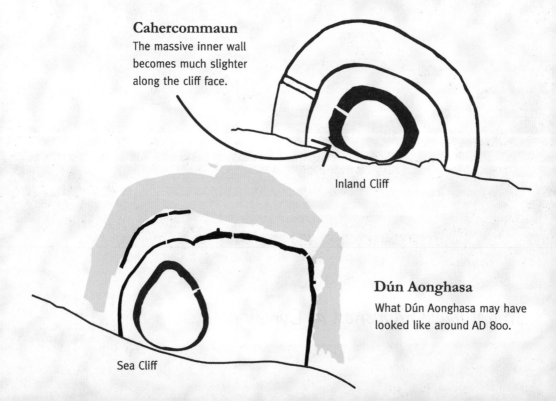

Cahercommaun

The massive inner wall becomes much slighter along the cliff face.

Inland Cliff

Dún Aonghasa

What Dún Aonghasa may have looked like around AD 800.

Sea Cliff

...What really happened at Dún Aonghasa.

Further Reading
····························

The Western Stone Forts project, volumes 1 and 2: excavations at Dún Aonghasa and Dún Eoghanachta, Aran Islands, Co. Galway. C. Cotter. Dublin. 2013. available from www.wordwellbooks.com

A study of the fort of Dun Aengusa in Inishmore, Aran Isles, Galway Bay. T.J. Westropp,. *Proceedings of the Royal Irish Academy*, 28C, 1-46. 1910.

Fresh insights into long-term environmental change on the Aran Islands based on palaeoecological investigations of lake sediments from Inis Oírr. K. Molloy and M. O'Connell. *Journal of the Galway Archaeological and Historical Society*, Vol. 59, 1-17. 2007.

The Book of Aran J. Waddell, J. O'Connell, J. and A. Korfe, (editors). Galway. 1994. (Includes a very detailed bibliography).

Oileáin Árann A. Powell. Dublin. 1984.

The Shores of Connemara S. Mac an Iomaire, Galway. 2000.

Nature Guide to the Aran Islands C. O'Rourke. Dublin. 2005.

An Aran Reader B. and R. Ó hEithir. Dublin. 1991.

Stones of Aran: Pilgrimage T. Robinson. London. 1986.

Stones of Aran: Labyrinth T. Robinson. Dublin. 1995.

Selected Poems; Tacar Dáinte M. Ó Direáin. The Goldsmith Press. Ireland. 1984.

The Selected Short Stories of Liam O'Flaherty L.O'Flaherty. London. 1992.

The Aran Islands J.M. Synge. 1907. (reissued in many editions).

Acknowledgements

Text: *Claire Cotter*
Layout: *Ian McCarthy*
Design: *Claire Cotter & Ian McCarthy*

Drawings

unless otherwise stated Ian McCarthy

Maps of the Aran Islands, and plans and drawings of Dún Aonghasa and Dún Eoghanachta based on originals by Sharon Weadick, Barry Masterson, Anthony Corns, Gary Devlin, Steve McGlade and the Dún Aonghasa and Dún Eoghanachta excavation teams. Finds drawings, John Murray and Tom O'Sullivan. Galway Bay 3D map, courtesy of Fabio Sacchetti, Infomar, www.infomar.ie; *chevaux de frise* map, Angel Esparza Arroya; Aran political map based on original in F.J. Byrne *Irish kings and high-kings*. Graphs: pg. 16 vegetation cover, based on originals by Karen Molloy and Michael O'Connell; pg. 68 livestock remains, Finbar McCormick and Emily Murray. Reconstruction drawings, cartoons and 'artoons': Conor McHale, pgs 17, 33, 77, 78, 92, 93 and 103; Paul Francis, timeline pg. 6 and pgs 34, 42, 47, 55, 100; Annie West pg. 105 anniewest.com; Anthony Corns, farm animals pg. 68; Cú Chulainn images, pg. 97, Will Sliney *Celtic Warrior: The Legend of Cú Chulainn*, The O'Brien Press Ltd, Dublin; 'Limpet Pickers' by E. Rivers, pg. 73, National Library of Ireland.

Photographs

Unless otherwise stated Claire Cotter

Front cover, Con Brogan, National Monuments Service, Dept of Arts, Heritage and the Gaeltacht; Dún Aonghasa image, pg. 3, George Row, aran.veryireland.com. Aerial photographs pgs 15, 26, 32, 58 and 90 and archive photo pg. 101, National Monuments Service, Dept of Arts, Heritage and the Gaeltacht; photo manipulation pg. 15, Anthony Corns. Fibula pg. 65, man fishing, pg.73, spearhead and axe pg. 79, brooch-pin pg. 93, National Museum of Ireland. Black & white aerial pg. 52, Irish Air Corps. Antiquarian photos pg. 39 and photo of Westropp pg. 101, Royal Society of Antiquaries of Ireland; Dún Aonghasa wall pg. 38, from Third Earl of Dunraven *Notes on Irish Architecture*, Vol. 1, 1875. 'Anthropometry in Aran' pg. 49, Trinity College Dublin collection, courtesy of Ciarán Walsh; 'Colm Mór Faherty' pg. 89, Sally and David Shaw-Smith; 'Boys on Aran' pg. 48, Jane Shackleton, courtesy of Chris Corlett. 'Polydactyly' pg. 71, Finbar McCormick; Guillemot pg. 75, Nicholas Jackson; Great Auk, pg. 75, Zoological Museum Trinity College Dublin. Finds photographs: Rose Cleary, Claire Cotter, David Jennings, Steve McGlade and John Scarry.

On the way down

The Aran Islands have a very mixed flora. Lime-loving plants, plants from Arctic - Alpine regions and plants that are normally found only in the warmer climes of southern Europe and the Mediterranean region all grow happily side by side. Here is a selection of some of the most common flowers you might see on your way to the fort. Please don't pick them - some are rare and very particular to the islands and the Burren.

Spring Gentian
Irish Name: Bláth Mhuire
Flowers mainly in late April and May

Wild Leek
Irish Name: Cainneann or Gairleog
Appears in early Summer, flowers in July.

Bloody Cranesbill
Irish Name: Crobh Dearg
Flowers throughout the Summer

Burnet Rose
Irish Name: Rós Fiáin
Flowers throughout Summer

Common Spotted Orchid
Irish Name: Nuacht Bhallach
Flowers in Summer

Fuchsia
Irish Name: Fiúise
Flowers in Summer and Autumn

Harebell
Irish Name: Méaracán Gorm
Flowers from Mid-Summer to Autumn

Honeysuckle or Woodbine
Irish Name: Féithleann
Flowers from Mid-Summer